Secret Walks
Cornwall

Secret Walks
Cornwall

by Rob Smith
With additional texts by John Payne and Alex Whittleton

First published by *Secret Seeker*, an imprint of One More Grain Of Sand, 2016
info@onemoregrainofsand.com

www.secretseeker.com

Edited by Alex Whittleton and Katie Halpin
Research by Steve Marvell, Brendan Barry and Rob Smith
Photography by Brendan Barry except where stated below
Design by Ben Hoo, Nicola Erdpresser and Rob Smith
Maps by Dog's Body Design, Chunning Chang and Rob Smith
Printed by Cambrian Printers, Aberystwyth, Wales

Photography credits: All photographs by Brendan Barry (www.brendanbarry.co.uk) except for the following. Pages 34–5, 44–5, 55, 90–91, 98–9, 116–17, 126–7 & 134–5 by Simon Bone; 43 by Mike Charles; 136–7 (also on back cover) by David Elliott; 74–5, 96 (also on front cover) & 146–7 by Helen Hotson; 42 by David Hughes; spine image by Daniel Kay; 16–17 (also on back cover) by Paul Nash; 154–5 by Malcolm Osman; 36–7, 40–41, 56–7, 60, 82–3, 88–9, 124–5, 126–7, 128–9, 132–3 & 140–41 by Rob Smith; 106–107 by Joan Veale; 26–7 (also on back cover), 62–3 (also on front cover) & 80 by Ian Woolcock.

A catalogue record for this book is available from the British Library.

ISBN: 978-1-910992-07-4

Help us update: More than two years, 1,000km and numerous pairs of walking shoes have gone into making this guide the best it can be, but if you think something could be improved, an instruction could be clearer or you find the perfect Pitstop to include in the next edition, we'd love to hear from you: info@onemoregrainofsand.com

Publisher's note: Many of the walks within this publication follow steep, rocky pathways, which may be seldom used and susceptible to erosion. Every effort has been made to provide sufficient warning where necessary. The publisher and author accept no responsibility for injuries or deaths that arise from following the routes featured in this book. You are responsible for your own safety – rely on your own assessment of whether a particular route is suitable for your abilities and whether it has deteriorated since publication of the book to a point where it is not safe.

CONTENTS

INTRODUCTION

From Arthurian legends and tales of smuggling to beautiful landscapes and dazzling stretches of coastline, Cornwall is held with affection in the hearts of the British 'staycationer' for many different reasons. But for a keen walker, the wild and bracing nature of the county's varied countryside is unparalleled.

Look at any Ordnance Survey map of the region and you will see an impressive network of green dotted lines encompassing more than 3,800km of marked trails, parts of which are the most challenging in the whole of the British Isles. Other highlights include the high moorland of Bodmin, with its deserved but long-denied national park status; estuaries and creeks brimming with water and pristine nature; and 480km of coastal footpaths with jaw-dropping views. In other words, Cornwall is a walking Mecca.

In this guide, we have picked out some of the lesser-known walking areas, offering you a chance to experience Cornwall's most secluded and peaceful countryside. Also in the book is a series of articles called the Extra Steps – one for each walk. We have chosen subjects that relate to each walk and we hope they will offer an insight into the real Kernow – a land that has long regarded itself as a nation apart.

THE COUNTRYSIDE CODE

RESPECT

When passing through farmland you should leave gates as you find them, either open or closed. Always follow the paths and avoid straying over planted crops when you are in fields. Never block entrances to fields, driveways or paths with your car – always find a safe and unobtrusive place to park, even if this means extending your walk by a few hundred metres.

PROTECT

Leave no trace of your visit and take your litter home. Keep dogs under close control at all times – a bad scare from a dog is enough to endanger the lives of valuable livestock. Always clear up dog mess and dispose of the collection bag or container properly.

ENJOY

Always plan ahead and be prepared for weather changes. Make sure you have enough daylight for the walk you are doing – with plenty of contingency time. Be sure to take note of any signage and warnings you see along the route.

HOW TO USE THIS BOOK

Important – read instructions carefully and stay on track
Cornwall is a fantastic place to explore on foot, and the routes within this book will take you to areas of the county that are wild and seldom trodden. At regular intervals we ask you to look for small, specific markers in order to find a pathway. This means you must be aware of your surroundings and make sure you read the instruction you are following fully (and ideally the subsequent one as well) in order to avoid getting lost. This is all the more important when walking and chatting with friends and family – it is easy to get distracted, misjudge distances and miss turnings.

Important for GPS users – estimated distances within the instructions
Rather than giving the exact distances recorded by GPS between reference points in the instructions, we have given rough distances and adjusted them very slightly according to the terrain. On rocky terrain it will always feel like you have walked further than you actually have, and so we have accounted for this.

The walk durations are based on a slow pace of 3km/hr with no stopping time.

ICONS AND TECHNICAL INFORMATION

Each walk has a series of icons that will give you important information about the route. Below is what they mean and how you should interpret them.

Max height
The maximum height the walk reaches above sea level

Total height gain
The total uphill walking during the walk

Walk difficulty
E = Easy
M = Medium
H = Hard
X = Extreme

Walk length
We have rounded this up to the nearest 0.5km

Walk duration
This is based on a pace of 3km/hr without stops

Walk addition with optional extras

Walk reduction with shortcut route

Panoramic views rated 1 to 5

Family suitability rated 1 to 5

Nature and beauty rated 1 to 5

MAPS AND MAP KEY

The maps we have created for the book should be used to give you an idea of where you are along the route and a sense of your surroundings. It is not possible to show every road and pathway at the scale we use, so don't worry if you see turnings not marked on the map. Simply follow the detailed written instructions.

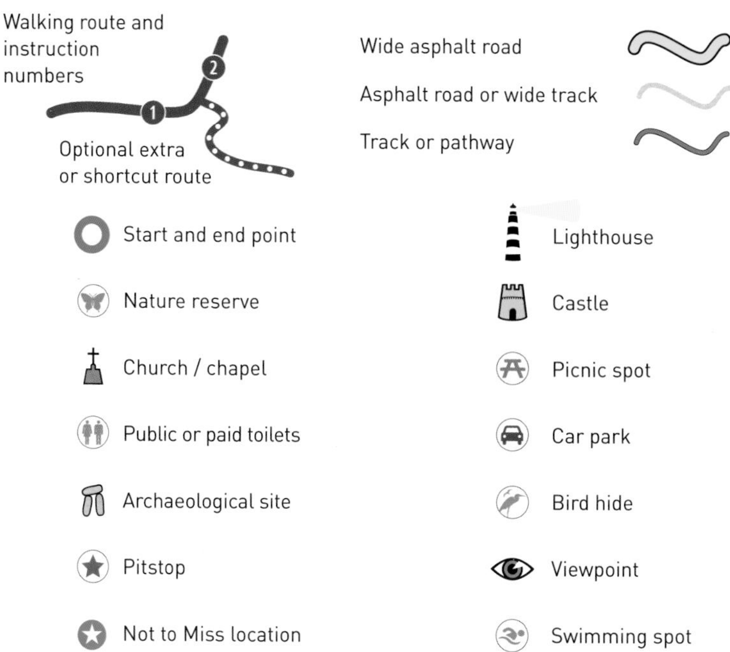

GETTING THERE AND DISTANCES

In the Getting There instructions we have used miles as our measurement of distance because users will generally be driving to the start points. However, in the walk instructions, we have used kilometres as our unit of measurement. This is because walking is gradually moving over to the metric system. (You will notice that new signs on pathways use kilometres and metres as distance measurements.)

The postcodes in the Getting There instructions are for sat-nav devices and will take the user to the nearest marked postcode to the walk start point.

THE EXTRA STEPS

The Extra Step articles in this book cover a range of subjects that include nature, history, architecture and ethnography. These short, accessible essays complement each walk – we hope they will make your time exploring Cornwall even more enjoyable.

THE PITSTOPS

The Pitstops in each walk are places to stop for refreshment on or near the walking route. A selection of pubs, restaurants and cafés have been chosen and even some delis or shops where you can pick up supplies for a picnic.

WALK LENGTHS AND LOCATIONS

No.	Walk	Grade and distance
1	West Penwith	Medium – 13km With optional extras – 15km Shortcut walk distance – 9km
2	Loe Valley	Easy – 10km With optional extras – 15km No shortcut
3	Black Head	Medium – 10km With optional extras – 12km Shortcut walk distance – 9.5km
4	Stithians Reservoir	Easy – 8km No optional extras No shortcut
5	Godrevy	Easy/Medium – 12km With optional extras – 20km Shortcut walk distance – 3.5km
6	Newquay & West Pentire	Medium – 11km With optional extras – 13km Shortcut walk distance – 9km
7	Dodman Point & Gorran Haven	Easy – 8km No optional extras Shortcut walk distance – 3.5km
8	Lansallos & Lantivet Bay	Easy – 4.5km With optional extras – 5.5km No shortcut
9	St Winnow & Lerryn	Easy/Medium – 7.5km With optional extras – 8km Shortcut walk distance – 5.5km
10	Cadson Bury Hill	Easy – 2.5km No optional extras Shortcut walk distance – 1km
11	Blisland	Hard – 7km No optional extras Shortcut walk distance – 4km
12	Fox Tor & East Moor	Medium – 7km No optional extras No shortcut
13	Trebarwith & Tregardock	Hard – 12.5km With optional extras – 13.5km Shortcut walk distance – 8km
14	Boscastle	Hard – 10.5km No optional extras Shortcut walk distance – 6.5km
15	Poundstock & Millook Haven	Easy – 6.5km With optional extras – 8km No shortcut

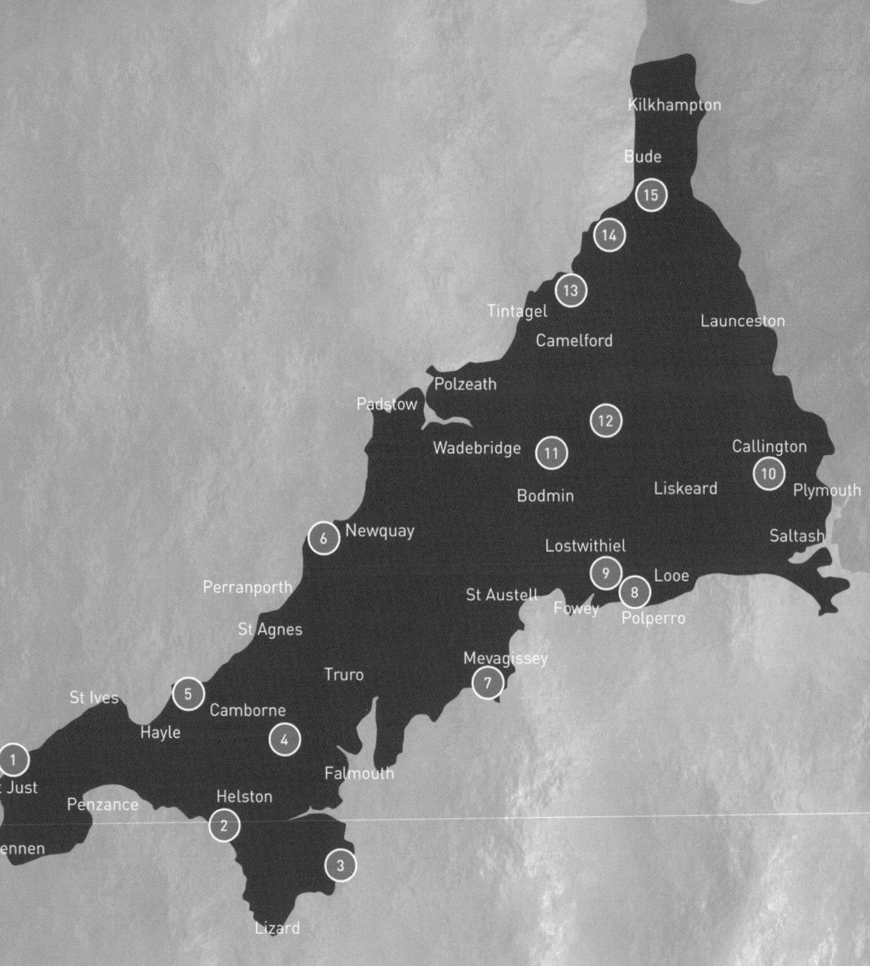
Kilkhampton
Bude
15
14
13
Tintagel
Launceston
Camelford
Polzeath
Padstow
12
Wadebridge
11
Callington
10
Bodmin
Liskeard
Plymouth
6
Newquay
Saltash
Lostwithiel
9
Looe
8
Perranporth
St Austell
Fowey
Polperro
St Agnes
Mevagissey
7
Truro
St Ives
5
Camborne
Hayle
4
1
Falmouth
Helston
Penzance
2
3
Lizard

West Penwith

Land of history, mystery and myth

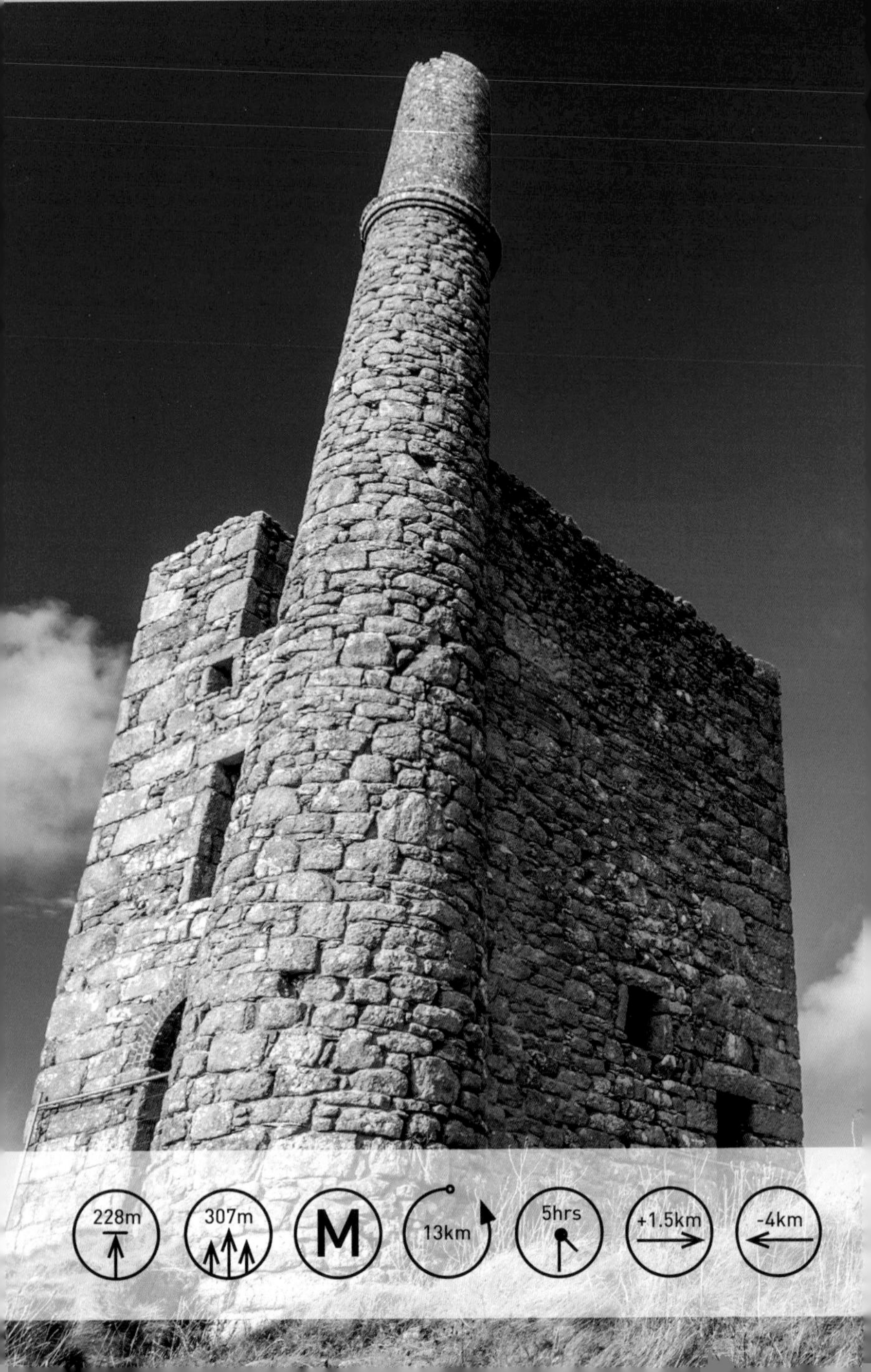

An invigorating walk in the westernmost reaches of Cornwall seems the perfect place to kick off any walking holiday in the county – and indeed to start this book. Our route leads you from the tumbledown granite remains of the Carn Galver mine, sweeping in a southerly loop through beautiful open moorland to the coastal parish of Morvah to the west. It's a great opportunity to visit some of the area's most mysterious and memorable monuments, including ancient standing stones and megalithic tombs. From the top of the immense rocky outcrop of Carn Galver, you can see both the north and south coasts of the Cornish peninsula in a breathtaking 360-degree panorama. If you don't fancy doing all of this fairly challenging route, there is a shortcut that knocks off roughly a third of the distance. Both options lead you up and down windswept hills, past isolated ancient ruins and along the dramatic coast path.

01

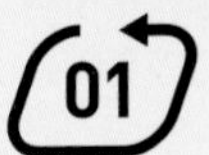

West Penwith

Land of history, mystery and myth

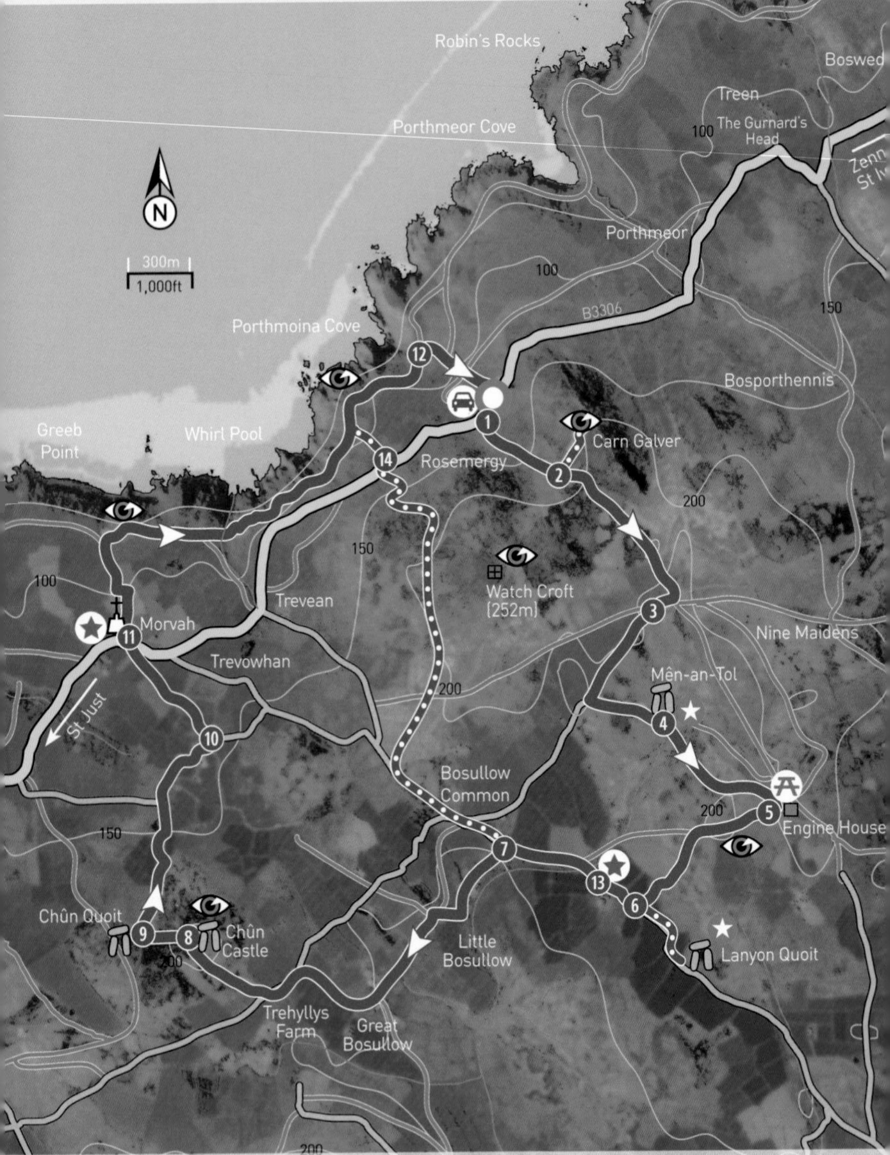

Gurnard's Head
Robin's Rocks
Boswed
Treen
The Gurnard's Head
100
Zenn
St Iv
Porthmeor Cove
N
300m
1,000ft
Porthmeor
100
B3306
150
Porthmoina Cove
12
Bosporthennis
Greeb Point
Whirl Pool
1
Carn Galver
14
Rosemergy
2
200
150
Watch Croft (252m)
100
Trevean
3
Morvah
11
Nine Maidens
Trevowhan
Mên-an-Tol
200
St Just
4
10
Bosullow Common
200
5
Engine House
150
7
13
6
Chûn Quoit
9
8
Chûn Castle
200
Little Bosullow
Lanyon Quoit
Trehyllys Farm
Great Bosullow
200
Higher Bodinnar
200
B3318
Newbridge

CLIMBS

225m
200m
175m
150m
125m
100m
0m
2km
4km
6km
8km
10km
12km
14km

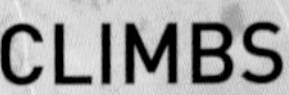

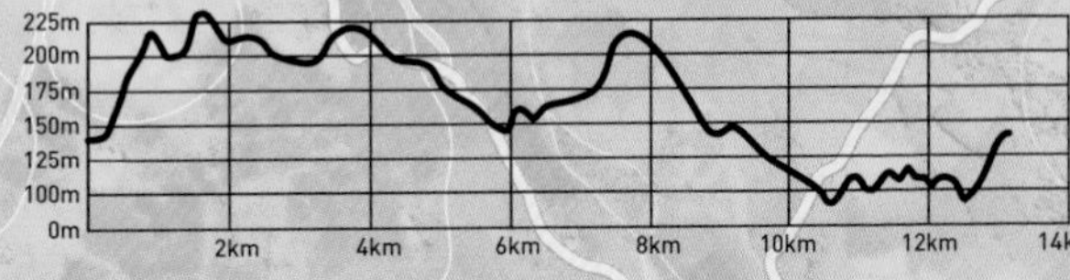

GETTING THERE

On the road from St Ives to St Just (B3306), between Zennor and Morvah, park at the Carn Galver mine ruins. They are unmarked from the road but easily recognisable from their shape – two large granite ruins separated by 20m, one with a high chimney. TR20 8YX.

WALK DIRECTIONS

❶ Before setting off, take a note of the shape and size of the Carn Galver rocks up on the hill and also the mine ruins – you will be asked to recognise them on your return. From the car park, turn right and walk along the B3306 for about 150m. Turn left onto the footpath just after the cattle grid. Follow the meandering path (indistinct in winter) uphill.

OPTIONAL EXTRA – When you're almost at the top of the hill, take the path to the left that leads up to the saddle-shaped rock of Carn Galver (SW425363). From here, the panoramic views of the surrounding countryside and coasts are stunning. (A there-and-back of about 750m.)

❷ Carrying on the route, head up and over the hill. After a while you will have hedges on each side of you. When the hedges end at a junction, turn right and follow for 100m or so, then fork left onto the main track.

❸ Follow this track for 500m or so, until you see a stone slab over a ditch on your left. Go over this and then the granite stile. 200m or so along this well-worn path you will pass the ancient (and mystical) stones known as Mên-an-Tol.

NOT TO MISS

Mên-an-Tol

The prehistoric rock formation Mên-an-Tol (Stone of the Hole) comprises several small upright stones, one of which has a large round hole in the middle. One of only two ancient 'holed stones' in Cornwall (the other is located on the Lizard Peninsula), this site has a solid place in local folklore. Legend has it that a piskie (Cornish for 'pixie') who could perform magical cures guarded the stone. By crawling through the hole a certain number of times many ailments could be cured, from infertility to rickets. (SW426349)

❹ After the stones, continue on the path for a kilometre or so, heading in the direction of – and until you reach – the Engine House (SW434345).

NOT TO MISS

Lanyon Quoit

This Neolithic burial chamber, which was once so tall that a horse and rider could travel beneath it, was dislodged in a storm in 1815. It was later rebuilt at right angles to its original position, only 1.5m from the ground and with three upright stones instead of four. (SW429336)

5. After enjoying the magnificent views from the Engine House, to continue on the route go to the side with the chimney, walk down the short slope, turn right onto the track, then fork left over the stile onto the path after a few metres. You will be heading roughly west. After about 250m, go over the stile next to the metal gate and keep straight ahead, keeping to the right-hand fence line. After 100m, ignore the right turn through the gate and instead veer left, following the field border to the bottom of the hedge and then the path round to the left. Follow for a few hundred metres, then cross over another stile to the right of a gate. You will now be on a grassy track, which leads to a lane after 100m.

OPTIONAL EXTRA – If you fancy another dose of ancient history, turn left on the lane and follow the road for about 0.5km until you reach Lanyon Quoit, accessed via a granite stile after two sharp bends.

6. To continue the route, turn right along the lane, soon passing Lanyon Tea Room (see p.23) on the right. 250m or so past the tearooms, turn left onto a lane, signposted Little Bosullow.

SHORTCUT – To take a shortcut at this point, go past the turn to Little Bosullow and on up the hill. Skip to Instruction 13 to follow the rest.

7. Follow the lane to Little Bosullow – after 300m or so it bends around to the right and up a steep hill. At the top, keep going on to the gravel track which is marked 'private access – Gwel A Ves'. (This applies to cars only.) After 250m or so, go over the stile next to the white cottage. Keep going past Moorvue Farm and keep going again on to an asphalt lane for about 300m, to a T-junction. Now turn left towards Trehyllys Farm, where you should follow the signs up the hill towards Chûn Castle – there is a large granite stone next to the path after 50m.

8 At the top of the hill are the remains of Chûn Castle (SW405339), an Iron Age hillfort built some 2,500 years ago, the entrance of which is marked by two upright granite pillars. Take a moment to soak up the view of almost the entire route you have followed so far. To continue, leave the castle through these pillars and join the path leading past the single upright stone. You should be able to see Chûn Quoit, another stone remnant of ancient settlements, ahead of you.

9 There are five paths that meet at Chûn Quoit. Take the path immediately to the right of the one on which you arrived. (You will follow a barbed-wire fence on the left for a short distance.) Now follow the blue arrows down the hill to a track. Turn left, then at the crossroads turn right. At the bottom of the hill go straight on, until you join an asphalt lane.

10 At the first sharp right-hand bend, go over the stile and onto the path signposted Morvah. Follow the natural course of this old footpath over stiles and along field edges until you arrive at the road (B3306). Now turn left and, after a few metres, fork right towards Morvah church.

11 To visit our Pitstop in Morvah (see p.23), keep going past the church for 100m, but to continue the route, turn right onto a footpath just before the church. Follow all the way to the coast path, where you should turn right. Continue along the coast path for some time, enjoying the views of wild seas and disused mines.

12 After about 3km, you will reach a wide rocky valley and see Carn Galver and the mine ruins from the start of the walk. Follow one of the paths inland to finish the walk – there is a small network of pathways here, but you will be able to find a route up to the mine ruins easily enough.

THE SHORTCUT

13 Picking up from Instruction 6, walk past the tearooms (or turn right as you exit them) and walk along the road. (Ignore the left turn for the longer route after about 500m.) Walk to the top of the hill, where you'll see two tracks close together on the right-hand side. Take the second, between two granite pillars, signposted Garden Mine Cottage. The track hugs the perimeter of the property and passes some derelict mine buildings, where, if you look up to your right, you can see the high hill of Watch Croft (SW420357), which rises 252m above sea level; there is a narrow and convoluted path up to the top, but it's worth the diversion if you have time to explore. Back on the shortcut, passing the large disused buildings, the track continues downhill to the B3306. At the road, turn right and after about 15m take the footpath to your left.

14 Head downhill and go over the gate and stile, then follow the grassy track down towards the sea. Go over another stile, in the hedge to the left of the gate, then continue downhill. Just after passing a granite post on your left, follow the stone hedge of a small enclosure, where you should join the coast path. Turn right, ignore the two tracks to your left and bear right uphill, keeping the sea to your left. Now turn to Instruction 12 to finish.

THE PITSTOPS

Lanyon Tea Room

Situated in an old milling room built by a mine captain 200 years ago, Lanyon Tea Room is an atmospheric but somewhat draughty place to stop. Try the savoury tea (scones, cheese and chutney) or a slice of homemade cake, or even buy a jar of jam or marmalade to take away with you. Dogs and muddy footwear are welcome here.
Lanyon Farmhouse, Morvah Road, Bosullow TR20 8NY
Open daily 2–5. 01736 351273. www.lanyontearoom.co.uk

Morvah Schoolhouse

The Schoolhouse serves traditional home-cooked meals, including stews and pies, as well as cream teas and other treats. The building – originally a chapel, built in 1744 – was converted into a community arts hub in 1999. Today, there's an art gallery upstairs with stunning sea views and a craft shop downstairs. Dogs are welcome in the café.
Morvah, Pendeen TR20 8YT. Open Apr–Sep Tue–Sun 10.30–4.30, Oct–Mar Thu–Sun 11–3.30. 01736 787808. www.morvah.com

THE EXTRA STEP

DH Lawrence and Helen Dunmore at Zennor

West Penwith is a spellbinding jumble of rocks, prehistoric monuments, isolated villages, dramatic coastline and teeming flora and fauna, including buzzards and wildflowers. When English writer DH Lawrence and his German-born wife, Frieda, sought refuge here in the village of Zennor during World War I, the writer immediately fell in love with its wild and windswept situation: 'It is a most beautiful place', he declared. 'A tiny granite village nestling under high, shaggy moor-hills, and a big sweep of lovely sea beyond.'

It was in this inspiring setting that Lawrence finished two of his better-known novels, *The Rainbow* (1915) and *Women in Love* (1920). However, due to the increasingly anxious mood of war, the writer's open anti-military stance and Frieda's parentage, the Lawrences became outcasts and were accused of sending signals to German submarines just off the coast here. In 1917, military police arrived in Zennor and the couple were given three days

to leave. And so began their years in exile, travelling around the world in search of refuge. Years later, Frieda described what drove this wanderlust: '...like an octopus, with slow but deadsure tentacles, the war spirit crept up and all around us. Suspicion and fear surrounded us. It was like breathing bad air and walking on a bog.'

In her 1993 novel, *Zennor in Darkness*, Helen Dunmore reimagines the couple's years in Zennor. Set in 1917, this work of fiction interweaves the lives of Claire Coyne and her shellshocked lover, John William, with those of the Lawrences. A key scene occurs in Zennor church, when the fictional Clare meets the real-life Lawrence over the carved bench end of a mermaid, whose breasts and belly swell above her scaly tail. For Clare, the mermaid is a symbol of innocence – the Virgin Mary, Star of the Sea. For Lawrence, however, the carving is yet another reminder of the difficulties of human relationships and sexual desire. Ultimately, the book is about a community's fear of the outsider, which is heightened in a wartime world rife with secrets and suspicion.

02 Loe Valley

The legendary lake by the sea

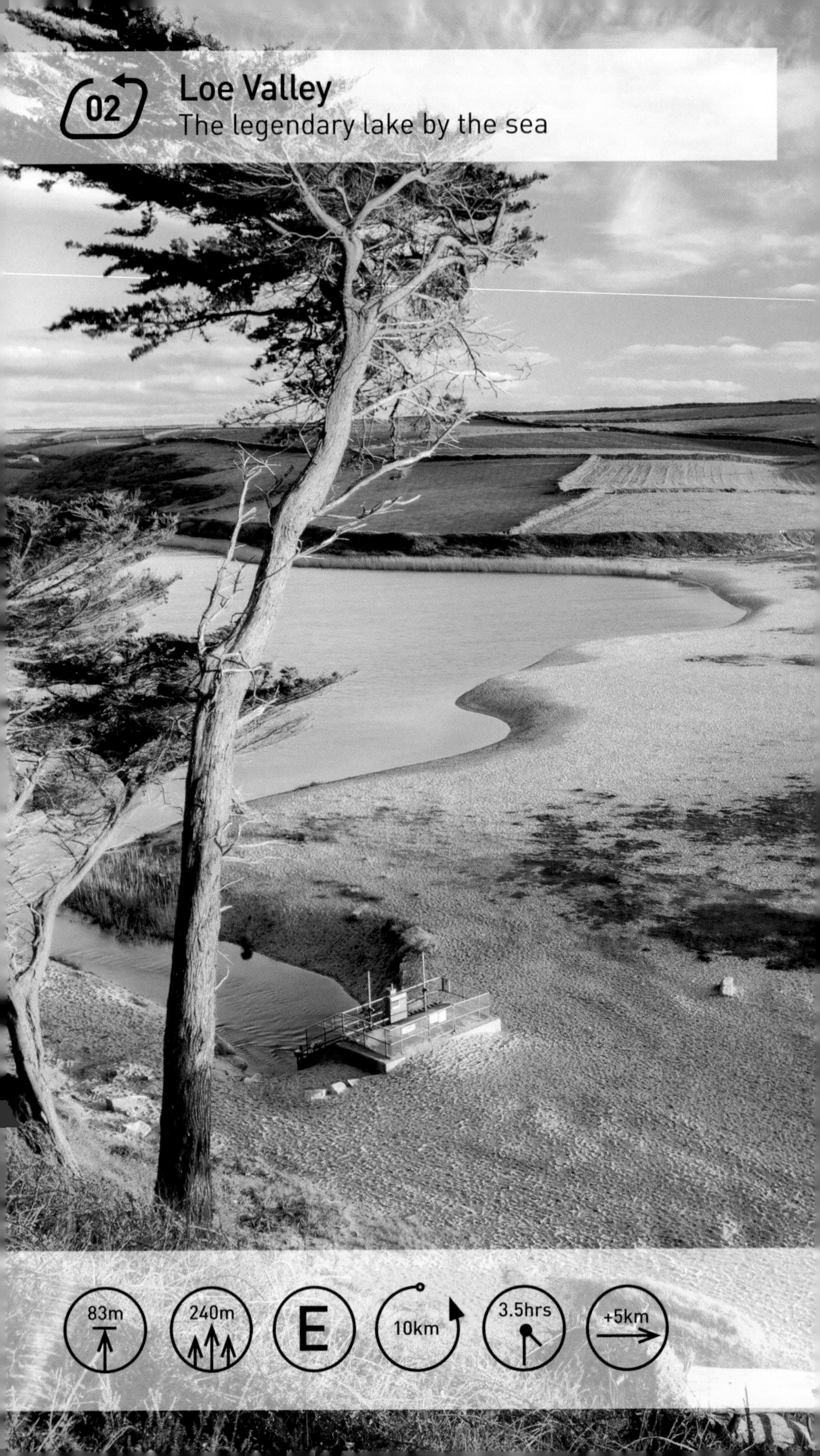

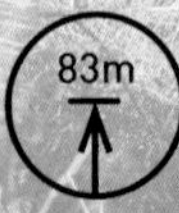

This is a long but gentle walk around Cornwall's largest natural freshwater lake, The Loe. Originally the Loe estuary, this body of water is now cut off from the sea by an enormous shingle bank, Loe Bar, which has been built up over the centuries by heavy Atlantic rollers. According to legend, this is the lake into which Sir Bedivere cast King Arthur's fabled sword, Excalibur. Wandering along its banks, you'll find plenty of quiet spots for a picnic beside the mythical waters. Meander through the wooded valley surrounding the lake, spotting wildlife as you go, before heading out onto the blustery shingle bank, with its stunning coastal views. End your journey with a well-earned rest at the National Trust Penrose estate.

02 Loe Valley

The legendary lake by the sea

CLIMBS

GETTING THERE

Follow the A394 into Helston town centre and find your way onto Porthleven Road (B3304). Park opposite the large boating lake, in the large (free) car park next to the garage. TR13 8SG.

WALK DIRECTIONS

1. Walk to the far end of the car park, join the short path to the left between the trees and turn right to walk along the concrete track. On this first stretch of the route, you'll encounter remnants of the county's mining heritage – the flues found throughout this part of Cornwall are the legacy of centuries of tin, lead and silver mining (see p.54).

2. After about 800m, the track bends sharply around to the left. Turn down the public bridleway on the right and then walk through the field to a gate, follow the path between hedgerows, go across a stream and through a second gate. You will now be on the lakeside pathway. There are a few offshoot pathways but it is easy enough to stay on the main path – simply keep the lake on your right and keep going. But don't miss out on the smaller pathways to the lakeside after 750m or so.

3. After 2km on this path, you reach a gate where you should continue into the field – again, with the lake on your right. After another gate you will arrive at a track, where you should turn right and continue, past the cottages, keeping to the lakeside pathway.

NOT TO MISS

Sea holly

Across the bar and in the surrounding sand, when in season, you'll find a curious looking plant that has bluish spiky leaves. It may look a little alarming for a wild food, but its roots can be candied to make a tasty snack.

NOT TO MISS

Picnic spots

Don't miss the various picnic spots along the route. On the eastern side, there's one about 750m after joining the lake pathway, where the path turns steeply uphill (there's a right turn to access this shady spot); the other is a sunnier location, on the right about 50m after entering the field in Instruction 3. We mention our favourites on the western side in Instruction 6. Tempting though it is on a hot day, swimming here is forbidden in order to preserve wildlife habitats.

Willow Carr

Wet woodland, or 'carr', forms in low-lying, poorly drained areas along riversides and streams – or where the water table is high. The Willow Carr here is of national importance because of the incredible range of plants and animals it supports. In the last century, there has been a general loss of wet woodland due to human activity (clearance and drainage works), but its importance is now being recognised and these areas are gradually gaining protection and reinstatement.

4 Soon after the cottage, you arrive at the tip of Carminowe Creek. Go right over the wooden walkway and fork right on the other side. (If the lake is flooded, take the higher path on the left.) Now simply walk the final 750m or so to the Loe Bar.

OPTIONAL EXTRA #1 – From the bar, you can follow the coast path (with the sea on your left) all the way to Porthleven and a Pitstop, the SeaDrift Kitchen Café (see opposite). It's a simple 5km addition to the route, with stunning coastal views. When you arrive in the town, ask for directions to the restaurant.

OPTIONAL EXTRA #2 – If you like the sound of the coastal views but don't want to walk all the way to Porthleven, simply walk in the other direction on the sandbar (with the sea on your right). Climb the hill to the small memorial cross on the eastern side of the beach – it's a lovely spot to admire the Loe Valley as well.

5 Continuing the route, cross the bar by walking to the right towards the house on the embankment. You will see a wide path leading uphill to reach it. Walk up to the house and make a sharp right turn to walk downhill on the track. This will rejoin the lake and take you once again into woods. You will notice exercise installations which are part of a 'green gym'.

6 After about 750m, you reach a bench next to the pull-up bars of the green gym. Look for the lower path down to the lake – this is a more secluded section with beautiful locations for picnics. This smaller path will eventually rejoin the main track around the lake.

7 Rejoining the main track, follow all the way to the Penrose estate and the second Pitstop on the route, The Stables (see opposite).

8 After The Stables, cross the lawn and creek area on the lane. Then turn right to continue on the lakeside track – now asphalt. 100m or so after the last building in the Penrose estate and passing through the gates, join the small path on the right to a bird hide. Veer left before the hide to follow a short but pretty section close to the lake. Again, this smaller path will soon rejoin the main path.

9 After a long section on the main lakeside track, turn right when you reach the small post. This will take you into the Willow Carr (see p.30) alongside the River Cober. Turn left onto the path before the bridge and walk along for a final 500m or so to reach a second bridge, which you should cross to find yourself back at the car park.

THE PITSTOPS

The Stables

Enjoy a cup of tea and a slice of homemade cake at The Stables. This rustic café, which is situated in a charming old stable building – as its name suggests – is popular with walkers, who make straight for the big tables out in the courtyard.
Penrose, Helston TR13 0RD. Open summer daily 10–4:30
01326 561407. www.nationaltrust.org.uk/penrose

SeaDrift Kitchen Café

Thought to be one of the finest places to eat in the area, SeaDrift Kitchen Café in nearby Porthleven has a contemporary menu featuring big breakfasts and lots of fresh fish. The atmosphere and décor are superb and the staff are friendly and knowledgeable.
Fore Street, Porthleven TR13 9HJ. Open Thu–Sat 10–10,
Wed 5.30–late. 01326 558733. www.seadriftporthleven.co.uk

THE EXTRA STEP

The Helston Flora ('Furry') Dance

Cornwall is lovely all year round, but particularly in the springtime, when splendid carpets of bluebells drench the landscape in colour, signalling winter's weakening grip. At this time of year, any chance to bid farewell to the long, dark days of winter and anticipate the warmth and bounty of summer is seized by the locals, who embrace traditional spring festivities with as much gusto as their ancestors did in times gone by. And little wonder, in a place that remains so in touch with its pagan roots and where nature and the elements still govern so much of life.

You need only look a few kilometres north of The Loe, to the market town of Helston, to see this seasonal merrymaking in action. Every year on 8 May, the streets of the town are decked out in bluebells, gorse and laurel leaves for the ancient Flora Dance, also known as the 'Furry' Dance to the locals; this is probably a corruption of the Cornish word 'fer', meaning 'fair' or 'feast'. This daylong celebration revolves around several dances, the first of which kicks off bright and early at 7am, and even at this hour, the townsfolk dress in their finery, the men wearing white shirts and ties and the women, summer frocks.

The local girls and boys also go to town with their outfits, dressing all in white for their 10am dance, flowers bouncing prettily from hair and buttonholes as they go. For the midday and evening dances, things get even more elaborate, with men donning top hats and tails and their partners, long dresses, hats and gloves. As part of each dance, in an ancient ritual that's said to drive out the darkness of winter and bring in the light of spring, participants weave their way in and out of shops, houses and gardens, accompanied by the popular song *Flora Dance*, which is played out by uniformed marching bands.

As part of the same event, the colourful Hal-an-Tow pageant moves up and down the streets like a modern-day history play, putting on re-enactments of historic and folkloric battles, including Saint George and the Dragon, Robin Hood and Little John, and scenes from the Spanish Armada.

Banned by the Victorians for its drunkenness and ribaldry, Helston's spring festival was revived in 1930 and has, since then, taken on a distinct air of Cornish nationalism. A proclamation is read in Cornish, many men wear the Cornish kilt and every mention of the county's patron saint, Piran, raises a cheer. To oil the celebratory wheels, Helston's very own Spingo ales flow throughout the day and long into the night at the Blue Anchor pub on Coinage Street, where they have been brewed for hundreds of years.

03 Black Head
Around the rocks the ragged rascal roams

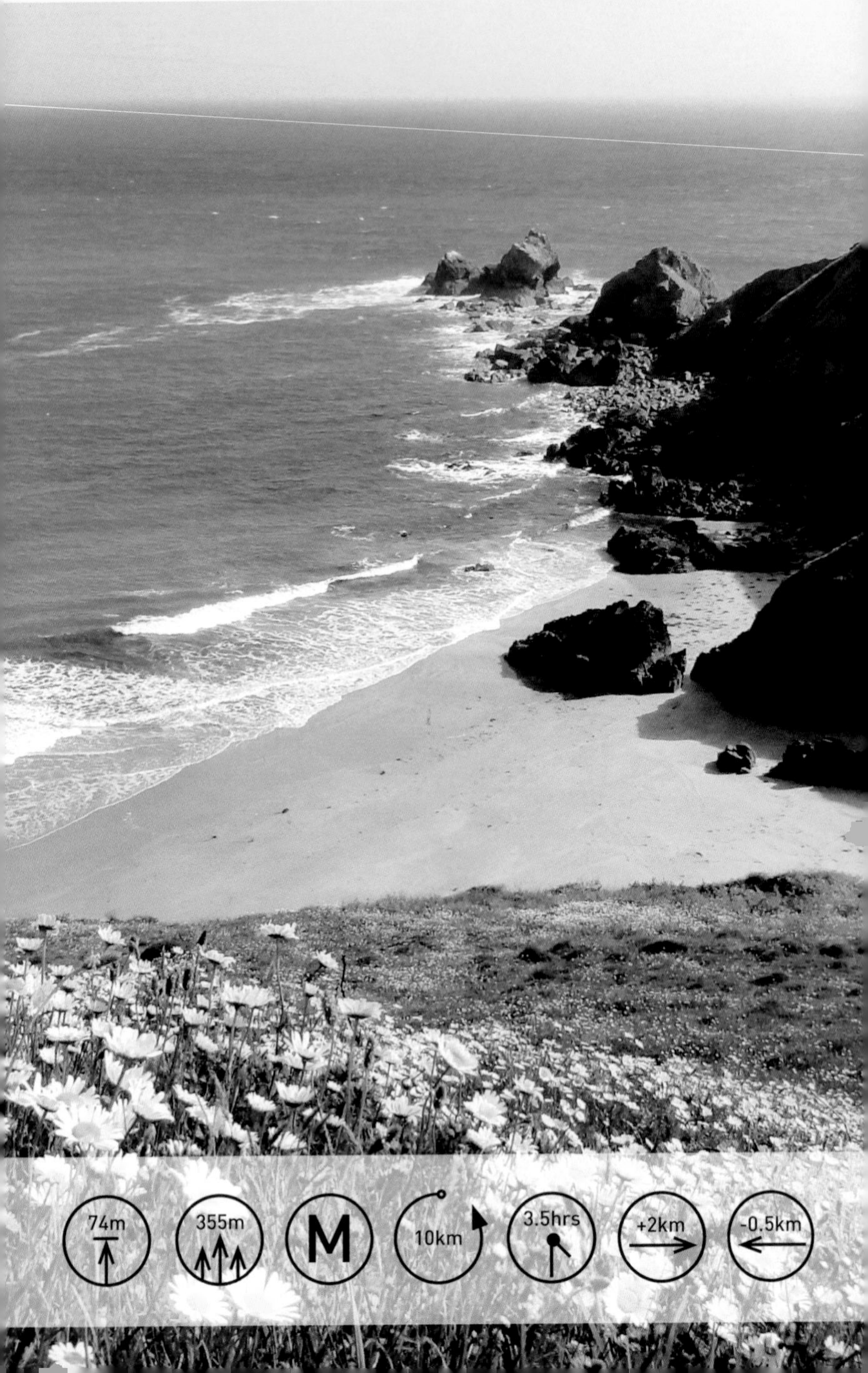

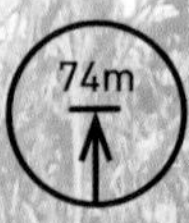

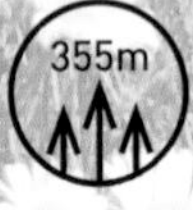

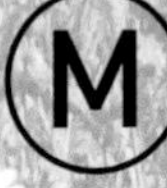

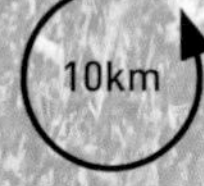

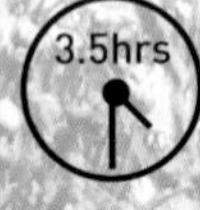

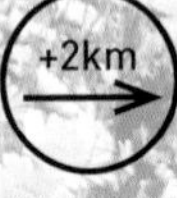

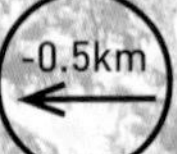

Skirting around one of the most southerly and unspoilt stretches of coastline in Britain, this walk offers sensational views. Keep your eyes peeled for dolphins and basking sharks, which frequently make an appearance just off the shore. There are three secluded sandy beaches along the way, framed by craggy rocks and lapped by water that turns an inviting shade of blue on sunny days. It can be a challenge to get down to them, but, if you manage it, you'll be amply rewarded with great snorkelling and bathing conditions. It's worth spending some time wandering around the picturesque harbour village and fishing port of Coverack before heading back across the fields to rejoin the coast path that heads back to the start.

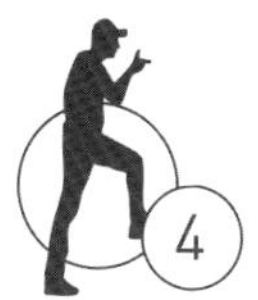

03 Black Head

Around the rocks the ragged rascal roams

CLIMBS

GETTING THERE

Head south on the B3293. Turn right at Zoar Petrol Station, a couple of miles after the radar dishes of Goonhilly. After about a mile, turn right to Ponsongath. Then after half-a-mile turn left at the Methodist church (a white building on the right) and follow the road for a mile. Park in a small lay-by on the left when you see the footpath sign – it's before the farm. TR12 6SH.

WALK DIRECTIONS

1. Take the track following the footpath sign past a house and go through a gate. When the track splits, turn left towards the sea. After the next gate, turn left and join the coast path. (Remember this point for your return.) Just here, if you walk straight ahead to the headland, you will find Lankidden Cliff Fort (see p.42) (SW755165).

2. Keep to the coast path, passing Lankidden Cove and the lovely Downas Cove – both featured in *Secret Beaches: Southwest England*. After a few kilometres, you'll meet a pathway junction – turn right. The next landmark is Black Head Lookout, a small white building at Chynhalls Point, where you have another there-and-back to a second cliff fort.

3. After the lookout, continue on the coast path and you will arrive at another junction. Our recommended route goes right here, taking you past Perprean Cove, but it is a rocky (and, at times, slippery) section. Keep going until you pass the cove and the coast path leads you along to the right. You reach a T-junction with an asphalt path.

SHORTCUT – If you prefer, you can take an easier route to avoid the rocky and slippery section. Instead of turning right in Instruction 3, simply walk past the large hotel on the headland by joining the path that leads straight ahead. You should find yourself following an asphalt path – look for the coast path on your left, which is where you rejoin the recommended route. (Keep going on the asphalt path to School Hill.)

4. Turn right onto the asphalt path and walk down to the lane – School Hill. Turn left, uphill, to continue the route.

OPTIONAL EXTRA – Turn right to walk downhill on School Hill and into Coverack village, where you will find our Pitstops (see p.43).

5. At the top of School Hill, after passing the school playing fields, go straight ahead onto a path on the right-hand bend. Walk through to the second field, where, after 75m, you turn left to go over the stile and walkway. In the third field, follow the right-hand edge to another stile and then make for the farm buildings.

NOT TO MISS

Lankidden cliff fort

This Iron Age cliff fort, which lies just off our route, once dominated the headland known as Carrick Lûz (or 'grey rock'). Like other cliff castles from this era, the earthwork defences at Lankidden comprised a bank (or rampart) and a ditch. It's thought that the fort would have had a ceremonial as well as protective function, and – given its position – it is likely to have served as an important trading centre. (SW755165)

6 Just to the right of the buildings, you will find a stile. Go over this and turn left to go through two large metal gates. This is a public right of way through Trewillis Farm. Follow the path past the buildings then veer right to join the driveway.

7 When you reach the lane, turn left then right after a few metres onto the footpath. Follow the telegraph poles across the field. In the next field, walk straight ahead to the corner.

8 Go over the stile, turn right and then immediately left onto the lane. This is Treleaver Farm. After 50m or so, veer right, avoiding the driveways, and follow the track to the dead end where there is a gate.

9 Go through the gate and walk to the coast path. Turn right and you will recognise your route from the beginning of the walk. After 1.5km or so, don't forget the right turn onto the farm track we asked you to remember at the beginning. Simply follow back to where you parked.

THE PITSTOPS

The Paris Hotel

Named after a liner that ran aground on local rocks in 1899, this hotel was built in 1907 and refurbished in 2012. Its Oceanview Restaurant offers excellent food and wine, as well as wonderful sea views, thanks to its three sides of windows. If it's a quick drink you're after, the hotel bar is ideal. The Cove, Coverack, Helston TR12 6SX. Open for breakfast, lunch and dinner daily. 01326 280258. www.pariscoverack.com

Archie's Loft

Perched right on the edge of the harbour in Coverack, this pretty whitewashed café sells hot and cold snacks, including pizzas and award-winning organic ice cream from local favourite Roskilly's. Enjoy spectacular views of the bay from the outside seating area on warm days. Cash only. The Cove, Coverack TR12 6SX. 01326 281440

THE EXTRA STEP

The Lizard, from shipwrecks to the space age

A lighthouse has dominated Lizard Point, the most southerly headland on the British mainland, since the middle of the 18th century. In former times and on clear days, sailors would also use the spire of nearby St Keverne church as a major navigational aid – the top of the spire can be seen from the Manacles, a set of treacherous rocks just beneath the surface of the waves near the hamlet of Porthoustock. Despite these guides for passing vessels, however, the Lizard's hazardous coastline has claimed many lives over the centuries, giving rise to its former nickname, Graveyard of Ships, as well as its modern-day reputation as an outstanding spot for divers.

One of the most popular wrecks for divers to explore is that of the SS *Mohegan*, a New York-bound steamer that ran off course and hit the Manacles one evening in October 1898. Due to the impractical position of the lifeboats on deck, 107 people went down with the ship, although the courageous crew of the Porthoustock lifeboat got there in time to save 44 people. One of the survivors was the captain himself, who fled the scene when he reached the shore. It's thought that he later committed suicide.

In the aftermath of the disaster, the parish of St Keverne opened its church for the laying out of the dead, and its houses to the families and friends of those who lost their lives. The Atlantic Transport Line, owners of the SS *Mohegan*, had a stained-glass memorial window made for the chancel of the church, and in the churchyard, a stone memorial was built to mark the communal grave of those who died that fateful night. It was a fitting response from a community that knows a thing or two about rallying for a common cause – St Keverne was, after all, the seat of the Cornish Rebellion of 1497, which saw 15,000 rebels march from Bodmin to Blackheath to protest unfair taxes imposed by Henry VII. The statue in the village of blacksmith Michael An Gof, leader of the uprising, serves as a reminder of this event.

But there's more to this weather-beaten peninsula than history. Since the 1960s, one of its most defining features has been a futuristic-looking cluster of gigantic 'golf balls' that make up the satellite-tracking station at Goonhilly Downs, now no longer active. In an incongruous but rather charming nod to the area's folkloric heritage, these high-tech dishes were named after characters from Arthurian legend – the largest is Merlin and the others include Guinevere, Tristan and Isolde – much of which plays out on Cornish soil. The site is to be redeveloped as a space-science centre – a fascinating, forward-looking enterprise in an otherwise primordial place.

04 Stithians Reservoir

Flora and fauna on a lakeside walk

234m

107m

E

8km

2hrs

04

It may seem contradictory, but a walk around man-made Stithians Reservoir will bring you very close to nature. The banks of this lake have been left largely wild and so support an abundance of birds, butterflies and other insects. The lake itself is home to many waterfowl and, if you're lucky, you'll be able to spot one of the area's indigenous birds of prey. The reservoir is also brimming with trout, which can sometimes be seen leaping out of the water. Go slowly and quietly to see as much of the area's teeming wildlife as possible. And don't be surprised if you notice the odd hedge or gatepost rising eerily from the water in times of drought. These are the remains of farms that lie at the bottom of the lake, which were flooded by the reservoir decades ago (see p.54).

04
Stithians Reservoir
Flora and fauna on a lakeside walk
Trewithen Moor
150
200
Penhalvean
Higher Nanpean
Lower Nanpean
Penhalveor
Tresevern
150
Penmennor
Tresevern Hill
Goonlaze
Hendra Ro
Higher Menherion
Tresevern Croft
Menherion
Carn
Carnmeor Farm
200
DAM
150
Yellow-wort
Stithians Reservoir
Carnve
Polmarth
Menerlue
PENMARTH
MENERDU
Polhigey Moor
Bird Hides
Polhigey
400m
1,000ft
CLIMBS
235m
230m
225m
220m
215m
210m
1km
2km
3km
4km
5km
6km
7km
8km
Halabezack
CARNKIE
150

GETTING THERE

If you're approaching from the north and heading towards the southern tip of the lake, you'll come across a small, unmarked car park just after Penmarth on your right-hand side. TR16 6PA.

WALK DIRECTIONS

1. Exit the car park, turn right along the road and walk for about 800m, until you see the gate for the bird hide on the right. Keep going over the low-level road embankment that cuts off the southernmost tip of the reservoir. On the other side, turn left onto the path through the mesh gate. Now simply walk along the eastern lake border.

2. After a good kilometre, you'll arrive at the reservoir dam. This structure holds back a staggering 5,200 million litres of water, supplying much of West Cornwall. Cross over the dam and turn left at the car park on the other side.

3. You will now be on a wide path – once again, on the lake border. Keep going for a couple of kilometres. About halfway along this stretch, you'll find a pretty bench, which makes an ideal picnic spot.

NOT TO MISS

Bird hides

For a really close look at the birds on the water, or for the perfect photo, try sitting quietly in one of the hides along the route. You'll find lots of information about the lake's birds and wildlife posted on the walls here. There's a hide just before the southern road bridge in Instruction 1 – to get there, pass through a gate and down a short path on the left-hand side of the road.

4. Towards the northern tip of the lake, the path bends around to the right and leads past a metal gate. Just before the gate, fork left onto a path to continue around the edge of the lake. After a few hundred metres, you will reach a road. Turn left and walk across another low-level road embankment towards the Golden Lion Inn (see opposite). Just before the pub, turn left onto the wide asphalt path.

5. Follow the path past the watersports centre, the public toilets, the car park and then, near the dinghy park, join the track. After another kilometre or so along the lakeshore, you'll see a standing stone on the right in a field. After this, you will walk over a small bridge and veer left. But after 100m or so, join the thin lane leading away from the lake on the right. (It runs between trees and goes slightly uphill.)

6. After 250m, turn left onto the grassy (unsignposted) bridleway. Walk to the end of this and turn right onto another narrow lane. Now simply walk the final 250m to the road. You will see the small parking area on the other side of the road, a few metres to the left.

NOT TO MISS

Dragonflies

The lake is known for its abundant dragonflies. It would be hard to identify all the different types – but you can try!

THE PITSTOPS

The Golden Lion Inn

This award-winning, family-run pub, which serves fine food and local ales, is the ideal place for lunch, supper or a drink after a long day exploring. The pub also has its own campsite and hosts monthly folk-music nights. Menherion, Redruth TR16 6NW. Open daily. 01209 860332 www.golden-lion-inn.co.uk

Caffe Nova

This café at the watersports centre sells tea, coffee, cakes and light lunches. It can get busy, especially at weekends, when big groups descend for much-needed refreshment after hours on the lake. To avoid the crowds, opt for the pub. Stithians Outdoor + Active Centre, Menherion, Redruth TR16 6NW. Open Mon, Thu & Fri 10–3, Sat & Sun 9–4 01209 862781. www.outdoorandactive.uk.com/location/stithians-lake

THE EXTRA STEP

Cornwall and the world

Beneath the boats and boards of the watersports enthusiasts who playfully skim the surface of this windswept lake lies 1.2 square kilometres of flooded farmland – a patchwork of fields, hedgerows, lanes and cottages that were submerged to accommodate the reservoir when it was built in 1967. As you stand at the water's edge reflecting on these forgotten farmsteads, take a moment to think about what else lies beneath the surface of the Cornish landscape, and very nearby – namely, the county's deep network of metal mines. These, which can be traced back as far as the Bronze Age, supplied raw materials and many of the engineering solutions that kept Britain at the forefront of the Industrial Revolution.

Stithians Reservoir is located slap-bang in the middle of Cornish mining country, sandwiched as it is between the mining centres of Gwennap to the northeast and Wendron to the southwest, and only a few miles from Camborne, with its famous School of Mines. Although the last of the working mines – South Crofty in Pool, near Camborne – closed in 1998, remnants of this local industry can still be seen in the form of the many engine towers that punctuate the landscape.

Cornish miners produced tin, copper, silver and other rare minerals, such as tungsten, which were smelted and turned into myriad objects, from pewter mugs for the local tavern to jewellery for the well-to-do. In the 18th century, the Cornish engine, a type of steam engine, was used to transport men and their machines to work and pump water from the mines. The invention revolutionised the industry, only to be replaced in the early 19th century with an even more efficient engine, designed by Cornish engineer Richard Trevithick, which went on to form the basis of the steam train.

In 1866, as a result of foreign competition, the price of copper collapsed. Although tin and arsenic continued to be extracted, many Cornish mines went out of business and countless families took their skills, technologies and traditions to far-flung places such as Australia, South Africa and North America, where they found themselves at the forefront of the global gold rush.

In 1930, the Old Cornwall Society was established to celebrate and sustain 'all those ancient things that make the spirit of Cornwall'. It has branches in towns and villages throughout the county and produces a newsletter that's become an important link between the county and its sons and daughters all over the world. The 'small ads' pages are full of messages from descendants of those long-dead mining families who are looking for the secrets of their ancestry, from every corner of the globe.

05 Godrevy

Carved otters and bathing seals

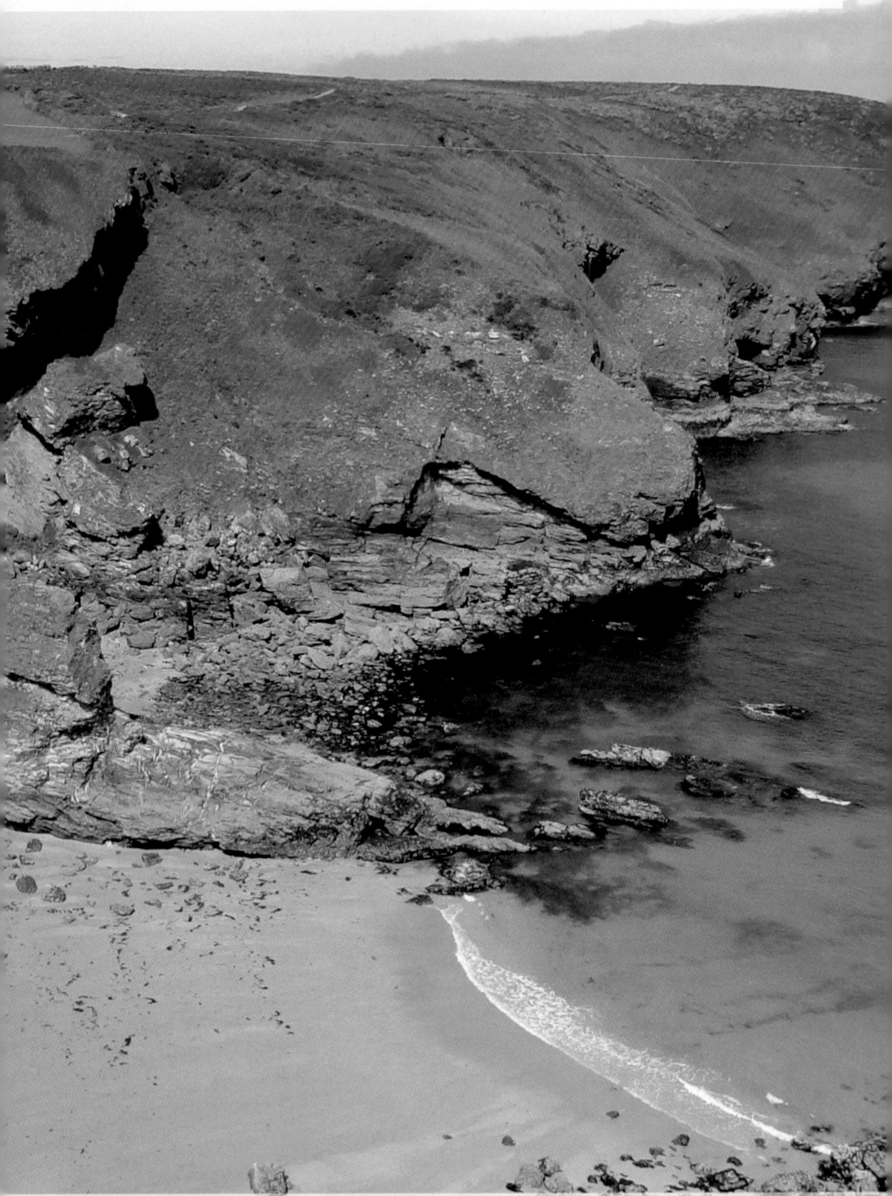

91m | 193m | E/M | 12km | 4hrs | +8km | -8.5km

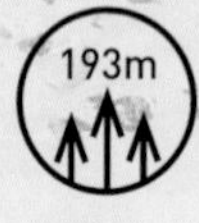

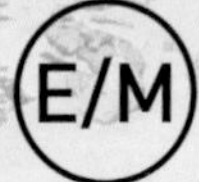

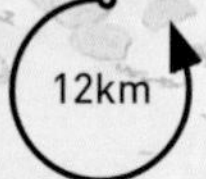

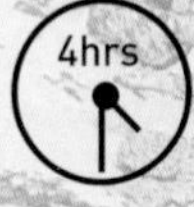

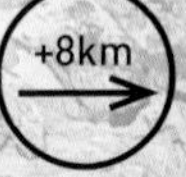

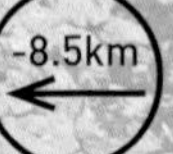

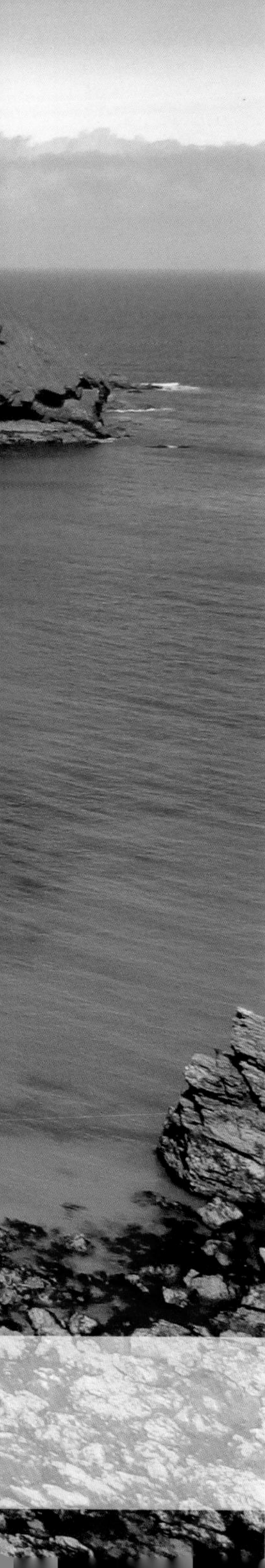

05

Taking in rugged coastline, pretty woodland and open countryside, this easy-going walk encompasses a plethora of natural wonders, including bathing seals, secluded beaches and a nature reserve. With clearly marked and well-preserved paths, it's one of the most accessible walks in the book, suitable for families and for those who don't consider themselves particularly athletic. That said, it's still a fairly long route with a couple of hilly sections, so you'll need a certain amount of stamina – and for those who feel the need for a challenge, the optional extra will be a welcome, hilly, addition. If you peer over the cliff edge on the lookout for seals, be careful – it's a long way down!

05

Godrevy

Carved otters and bathing seals

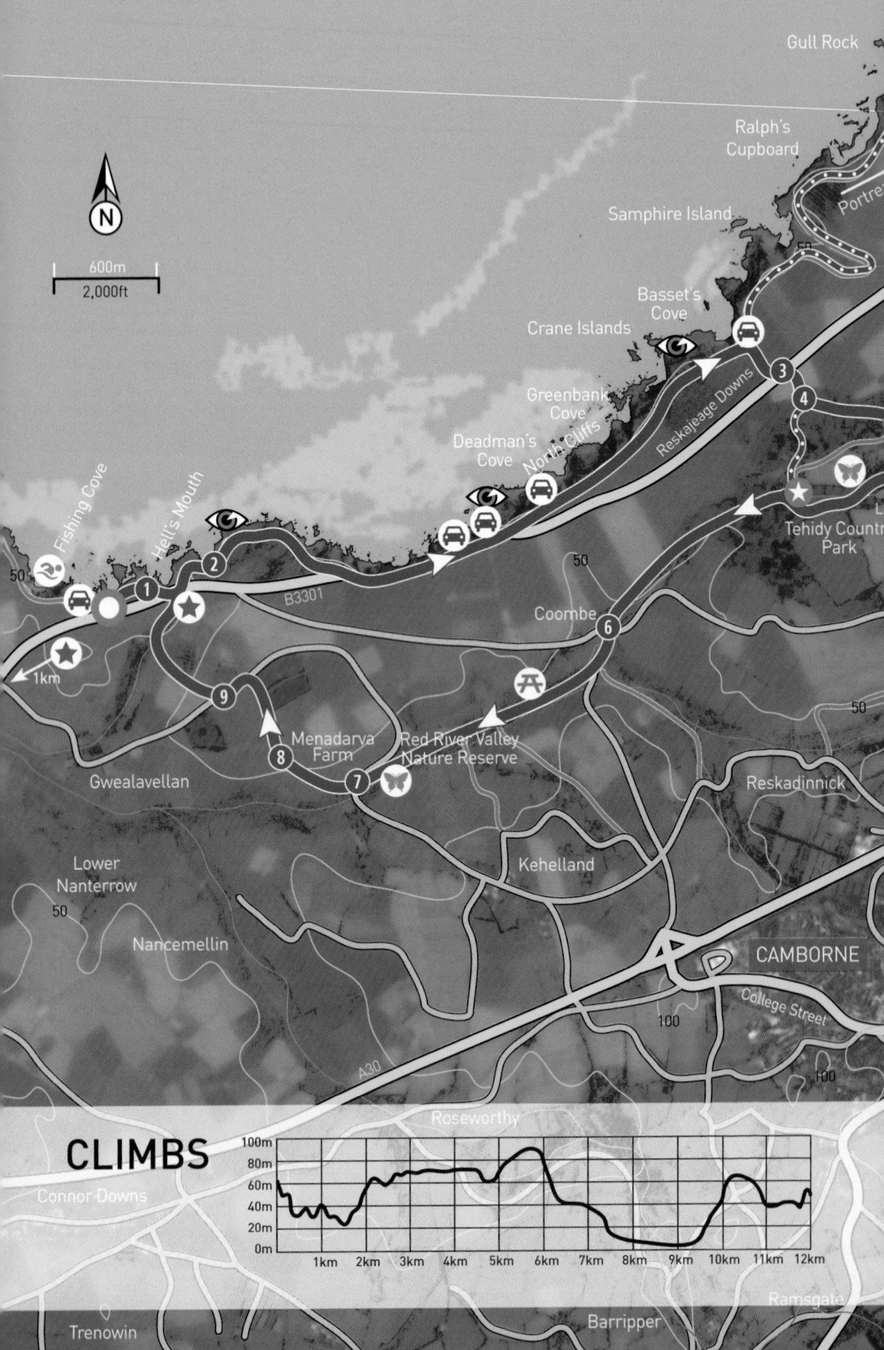

GETTING THERE

Follow the B3301 north out of Hayle, through Gwithian, past the Godrevy National Trust car park and up the hill. Park in the first car park at the top of the hill, on your left before the Hell's Mouth Café. If you're approaching on the B3301 from the east, the car park is on the right after the café. TR27 5EE.

WALK DIRECTIONS

1. From the entrance to the car park, take the footpath on the left through the bushes and head towards the coast. Turn right along the coast path; the sea will be on your left. Here, at Hell's Mouth, opposite the café (see p.61), pay attention – in among the surf and rocks below you may see a pod of seals.

2. Follow the coast path along the clifftops. After 2.5km, you will pass the first of four car parks. At the fourth, after a full 5km, turn off the coast path to head inland on the long, straight car park access road. Walk 250m to reach an asphalt road, where you turn left.

OPTIONAL EXTRA – This adds about 8km to the route and takes you along the coast to Portreath and then back inland, extending the walk to nearly 20km. Keep going on the coast path after the fourth car park in Instruction 2. It's about 4km to Portreath if you stay on the paths closest to the sea. (Be sure to cut inland to avoid the steep valley after 1km.) Once in Portreath, walk inland from the beach and you should find your way onto a pathway that runs south from the river and past Feadon Farm. Follow this around the house and then through fields to arrive at a road after about 1.5km. Cross over the road and follow the path into Tehidy Country Park and walk a good 1km past the golf course. Pick up the instructions from the end of Instruction 4 (turn left instead of right).

3. After only 50m on the road, turn onto the footpath on the right and walk 200m to the woodland where you meet a 6-way footpath junction. You are now in Tehidy Country Park. (There is a fairly extensive network of pathways and should you lose track of our instructions, simply find your way down into the valley and turn right to follow the stream.)

SHORTCUT (ALTERNATIVE START POINT)– This is a great option for families with younger children, as it cuts out the hills and a large part of the route. Start in the fourth car park mentioned in Instruction 2 – it's easy to find on the B3301 (heading east, it's 50m or so on the left after the Tehidy car park; heading west, 50m or so before it on the right). The shortcut is really just an exploration of Tehidy Woods and Tehidy Country Park. Simply follow from Instruction 2 to Instruction 5, then, instead of turning left to go to Coombe, follow your nose back up to the coast and the car park.

NOT TO MISS

Twisted tree

This large oak has an impressively twisted and gnarled trunk. Have a go on the rope swing if it'll take your weight.

Carved bench

Just before the left-turn to Coombe in Instruction 5, look for the pretty bench carved into the shape of two otters.

4. At the 6-way junction, take the path straight ahead (to the right of the sign) and follow the main course of this wide path. After a while, let it lead you right and slightly downhill to a wide (forked) T-junction. Go left to walk on a well-formed track with a wooden fence on your right. Look for the twisted tree after 50m or so on your left. Next you will reach a crossways. Go right and follow the track down to the gate (this is where the optional extra rejoins). Go through the gate and walk straight ahead on the asphalt road. A golf course should be on your left. After 100m, at the junction, join the path to the right, signposted Country Park.

5. When you reach the first path junction, go right and follow the main path past the lake. 100m or so after the lake, just after the small bridge, turn right onto the path that runs alongside the stream. Follow this down to the next bridge. Cross over the bridge and walk 50m or so to the junction. Turn left, signposted Coombe, and follow for about 1.5km.

6 When you reach it, turn left onto the road in Coombe and walk to the T-junction. Turn right and follow the edge of the asphalt lane, next to the stream, for 100m. Then go over the small bridge on the right to join the bridleway. You are now in the Red River Valley Nature Reserve. As you walk along, after 500m or so, you'll see small tracks on your left leading to the Red River – this name comes from the mineral deposits associated with tin mining, which in past times coloured the water red. (The colour is still visible in long-standing puddles in the winter.)

7 After 1.5km, you reach a stream and a narrow lane. Go over the stepping stones and left onto the lane. After 50m, go right, uphill, on a public footpath (also the driveway for Menadarva Farm). Walk past the farm (on your right) and after the last building, you will see a metal gate straight ahead. Go through this, then uphill across the field to the gates at the top.

8 Go through the gate on the right and follow the right-hand field edge uphill to a stile. Go over this and follow the edge of the next, quite large, field to a stone stile and farm lane. Turn left.

9 After 150m (just after the large barn on your left), join the public footpath on the right – go through the gate and walk along the right-hand field edge. Pass over the broken stile next to another gate and continue downhill towards the woods. Go through another little gate and into the woods; it can get a little muddy here, so watch your step. On the other side of the woods, turn right at the stone house and follow the track to the Hell's Mouth Café. Cross the road carefully and turn left back along the coast path towards the parking area and your car.

THE PITSTOPS

Hell's Mouth Café

This beach café and bar serves excellent breakfasts, light lunches and afternoon teas. Expect great background music here, too. Gwithian TR27 5EG. Open daily. 01209 718419

Godrevy Beach Café

Right on the beach at Godrevy, this cheap and cheerful café is the place to go for a hot chocolate or a big meal after a chilly surf. Gwithian, Hayle TR27 5ED. Open Feb–Oct daily, Nov–Jan reduced hours. 01736 757999. www.godrevycafe.co.uk

THE EXTRA STEP

Virginia Woolf in St Ives Bay

Godrevy Lighthouse is widely acknowledged to have been the inspiration for Virginia Woolf's famous novel *To the Lighthouse*, even though the work is set on the Isle of Skye in Scotland's Inner Hebrides. Clearly visible all the way across St Ives Bay, the distinctive white tower was familiar to the author from happy childhood holidays playing on nearby Upton Towan beach, part of the Towans – a 5km stretch of sand dunes fringing this section of the bay. Virginia Stephen, as she was then, first visited this spot with her family in 1892, at the age of 10, but stopped coming at the age of 13, after her mother died. The young Virginia signed the visitors' book in the lighthouse on her first visit. The book sold at Bonhams in 2011 for a staggering £10,250.

The striking 26m-high octagonal tower that made such a lasting impression on this giant of the Modernist period was built in 1858–59 on the largest rock of the hazardous Stones reef, along with two keepers' cottages. Locals had campaigned for its construction for many years, feeling all too keenly the need to warn mariners of the deadly reef, but it was only when the steamer SS *Nile* and her 40-strong crew went down here on a stormy night in 1854 that officials finally sat up and listened.

Originally, the light in the tower was manual, operated by a team of two keepers, but it was automated in 1939. In 2012, the light was switched off within the tower and replaced with a powerful LED mounted on a steel structure on an adjacent rock. Despite its lack of use, the Grade II-listed landmark is still maintained by Trinity House, the Official Lighthouse Authority, as a day mark for passing ships. It is hoped that this important piece of Cornwall's maritime and literary heritage will be protected and preserved for future generations.

Newquay and West Pentire

Surf's up!

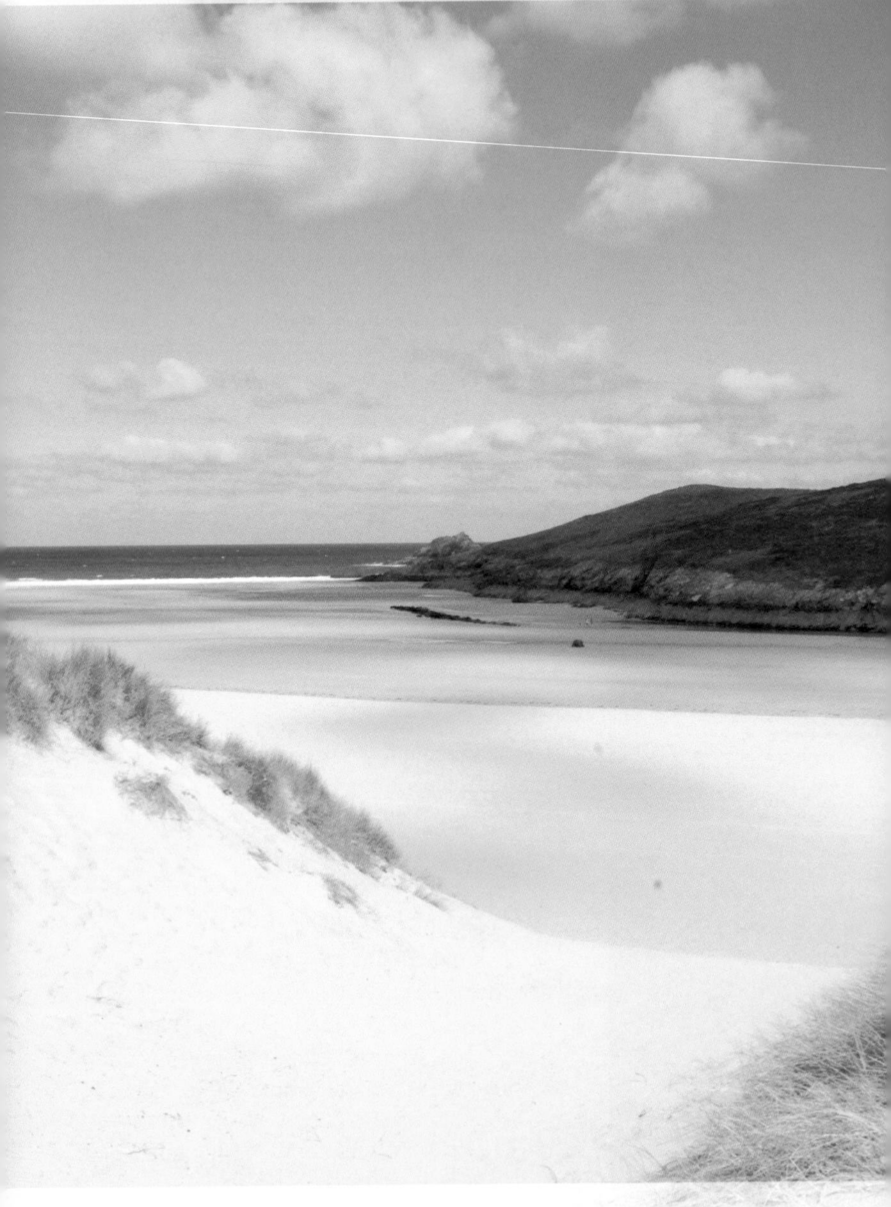

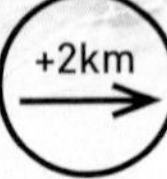

06

This walk along the coast to the south and west of Newquay will lead you across a tidal river, up and over sand dunes, into a sea cave and to a delightful swimming beach known as Polly Joke – and that's all before the halfway point. A little way inland on the loop back round to the start lies the quaint village of Crantock, with its tearoom, country pubs, traditional red phone box and small, vibrant art gallery displaying works by local artists. Back on the eastern side of the river estuary, you can look down on surfers catching waves on world-famous Fistral beach. Be sure to embark on this walk on a falling tide, as the river can only be crossed on foot at low water. However, if you mistime things, don't worry unduly – we've given you two optional high-tide return routes.

06

Newquay and West Pentire

Surf's up!

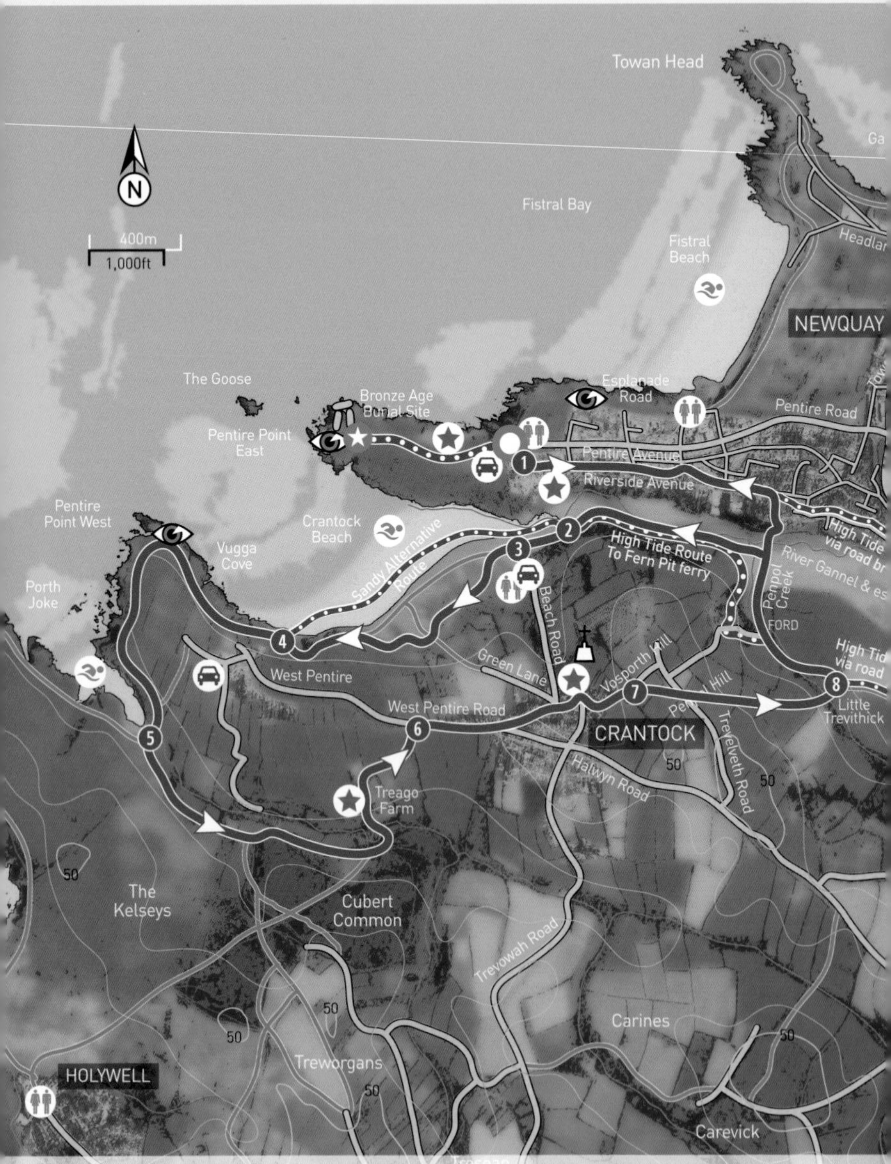

Towan Head
N
400m
1,000ft
Fistral Bay
Fistral Beach
NEWQUAY
Headland
The Goose
Bronze Age Burial Site
Esplanade Road
Pentire Road
Pentire Point East
Pentire Avenue
Riverside Avenue
Pentire Point West
Crantock Beach
Vugga Cove
Porth Joke
Sandy Alternative Route
High Tide Route To Fern Pit ferry
High Tide via road
River Gannel & estuary
Penpol Creek
FORD
Beach Road
Green Lane
West Pentire
West Pentire Road
Vosporth Hill
Trevelveth Road
Little Trevithick
CRANTOCK
Halwyn Road
Treago Farm
The Kelseys
Cubert Common
Trevowah Road
Carines
Treworgans
HOLYWELL
Carevick
Tresean
Ellenglaze Lane
CUBERT
1
2
3
4
5
6
7
8
50

CLIMBS

100m
90m
80m
70m
60m
50m
1km
2km
3km
4km
5km
6km
7km
8km
9km
10km
11km

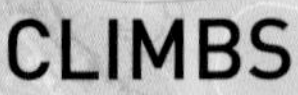

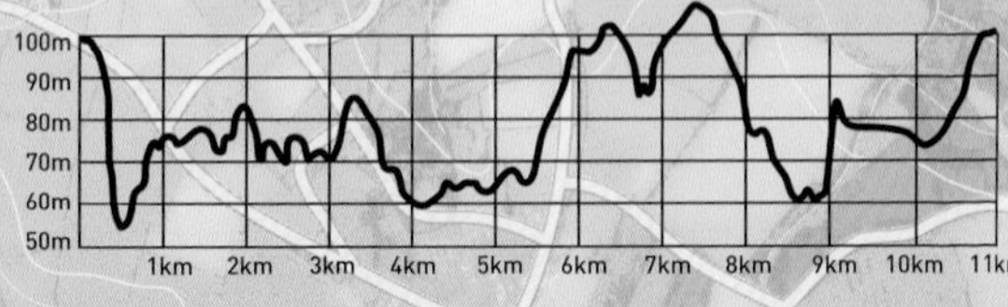

GETTING THERE

Follow Trevemper Road and then Gannel Road (A392) into Newquay and then follow signs to Pentire. You'll be on Pentire Road, which turns into Pentire Avenue. Park in the car park at the far end of the road. TR7 1QD.

IMPORTANT – ESTUARY CROSSING: The walkway across the Gannel estuary mentioned in Instruction 1 is passable from 3 hours before to 3 hours after low tide. Outside these times, the tide will cover the walkway and sand around it. But we have two alternatives. The first is to cross to and from the Fern Pit Café and Ferry, which has a private ferry that will take you across when the tide is too high for the walkway crossing. However, this only operates in summer, from Whit Sunday until mid-September (10–6). The second alternative is to start the walk at Crantock beach car park – this is shown on the map and featured in the instructions as the shortcut for this walk.
HIGH-TIDE RETURN: If you should arrive back at the estuary and the tide is in too far to cross at the walkway, walk down to the road bridge (see map) or, if in summer, use the Fern Pit ferry.

WALK DIRECTIONS

1. Exit the car park the way you came in and turn immediately right onto the small lane heading downhill – this is Riverside Avenue. Follow the left-hand bend and walk past the first Pitstop, Fern Pit Café and Ferry, featured in *Secret Kitchen: Southwest England*. This is also the optional summer estuary crossing – see above. After 150m, at the sharp left-hand bend, turn right onto another small lane heading downhill. Keep walking straight ahead to join a road and until you reach a T-junction. Turn right and, after 25m or so, right again onto the wide path that will take you down to the estuary. You will see the walkway ahead of you.

2. Cross the walkway and walk back along the sand towards the sea. You will see where Penpol Creek enters the estuary on your left and, closer in to the centre of the estuary, a small rocky promontory and a field above it. Go over to this point and up the steps carved into the rock. Follow the path along the field edge and into the woods alongside the estuary. Stay on the path and then walk straight ahead when you reach the track with houses on your right. After 150m, turn left back onto the coast path and down the steps to Crantock beach car park. (A sandy, low-tide alternative here is to walk along the estuary and over to the steps on the far side of Crantock beach, then rejoin at Instruction 4.)

SHORTCUT (ALTERNATIVE START POINT) – By starting the walk at Crantock beach car park, you will shorten the route by about 3km. Pick up from Instruction 3 to start the walk and add Instruction 2 to the end of the walk (when you arrive back at Penpol Creek in Instruction 8).

3. On the opposite side to where you entered Crantock beach car park, you will see the continuation of the coast path – go through the gate and follow. (If you are starting the walk here, join the path on the left as you face the estuary.) Walk up to the dunes and follow the posts across to the defined path that leads inland just near the first house – after 50m or so, make sure you turn right to stay on the coast path.

4. Now follow the coast path for at least 500m. You will pass some steps (final exit from the sand, if you have taken the sandy alternative route), after which are some crop fields. At the junction, go right and through the kissing gate. Then, after 100m or so, stay on the coast path by walking over the hill or take the short detour to Vugga Cove and then walk along the lower path around the headland.

5. Soon you will see a long sandy inlet on your right and, after about 500m, you will arrive at its inland tip – this is Porth Joke (named Polly Joke by locals). Turn left onto the path heading inland, signposted Cubert Common. Follow this all the way to the small car park and go through the two gates and over the stream. Turn left onto the track and keep following through the gates as the track turns into asphalt and leads you through Treago Farm holiday park. Don't miss our second Pitstop here, Treago Farm Shop (see opposite).

6. A while after the holiday park, you arrive at a T-junction. Turn right and walk 250m or so into Crantock. Just as you arrive, fork left onto the lane when you see Paul's Bench. Keep walking, mostly downhill, to a T-junction. Turn right again and walk into the village square to find another Pitstop, Cosy Nook Tea Gardens (see opposite). On the far side of the square to where you arrived, and directly opposite the traditional red phone box, walk uphill on the small lane, Vosporth Hill.

7. After about 250m on Vosporth Hill, go up the small steps to join the pathway that's just after a driveway on your right. Walk on the path through two fields and then straight over the lane. In the field after the lane, fork right and then in the next field, walk straight across to the bottom corner to join a hidden path within the hedgerow. When you come out into a field, walk towards a slate-roofed house. As you near the bottom of the steep hill, bear right and look for the stile. Go over this, then over the bridge and through some gates to find yourself on a track.

HIGH-TIDE ROUTE: If you arrive at this track more than 3 hours after low tide, the chances are that the walkway in the estuary will be submerged. (Although it's worth checking, if your timing is close, as at certain times of year the tide heights vary). If you need to, turn right at this point on the route and follow the track to the road bridge to walk back on the other side. (Or, if in summer, you can use the Fern Pit ferry.)

8 Assuming you are within 3 hours of low tide, turn left, walk downhill on the track, follow round the bend and then through two large metal gates. You will find yourself at a fjord – this is Penpol Creek. Walk along the path next to the creek and down onto the sand. The walkway will be ahead of you. Follow the same route back to the car park. (After walking up the path on the far side of the estuary, turn left then left again. Follow Riverside Avenue straight ahead at two junctions and up the hill, to walk past the Fern Pit Café and Ferry and back to the start.)

NOT TO MISS

Bronze Age burial site

To end the walk, take the time to visit the remains of the Bronze Age burial site at the tip of Pentire Point East, which dates from around 1500 BC. Although now a little eroded, this 10–12m-wide structure must once have been a fine barrow. While you're here, look out for the headland's many nesting birds, including skylarks and stonechats. (SW781615)

THE PITSTOPS

Fern Pit Café and Ferry

From this fantastic vantage point, enjoy cream teas, homemade cakes and sandwiches generously filled with prawns and freshly caught crab.
19 Riverside Crescent, Pentire, Newquay TR7 1PJ. Open summer daily 10–5, winter times vary. 01637 873181. www.fernpit.co.uk

Treago Farm Shop

Perfectly positioned at just over halfway around the walk, this well-stocked farm shop has an on-site bakery that sells homemade pasties and other treats. It also offers takeaway evening meals and, if you're lucky, hearty Sunday roasts in winter – call ahead to reserve a roast.
Crantock, Newquay TR8 5QS. 01637 830277. www.treagofarm.co.uk

The Cosy Nook Tea Gardens and Restaurant

It's said that this superb little tearoom serves up the best scones in the area. Expect friendly staff, a warm welcome for dogs and a small contemporary art gallery showcasing works by local artists.
Langurroc Road, Crantock, Newquay TR8 5RB. Open daily. 01637 830324

Lewinnick Lodge

Overlooking Fistral beach from a commanding sundeck, this dog-friendly hotel and restaurant offers twice-daily changing fish and seafood specials.
Pentire Headland, Newquay TR7 1QD. Open daily. 01637 878117
www.lewinnicklodge.co.uk

THE EXTRA STEP

The food of Cornwall

When you think of Cornwall, images of fresh fish and seafood, golden-crusted pasties and scones piled high with jam and clotted cream immediately spring to mind. The cuisine in this largely rural county is almost entirely shaped by its three sides of swirling sea, as well as its wet climate and poor-quality soil, which make the landscape better suited to growing pasture for grazing meat and dairy cattle than for arable crops.

Ever since Tudor times, Cornwall has had a thriving fishing industry, and Newlyn, to the west of Penzance, remains one of the most productive fishing ports in Britain. There can be little doubt that superb seafood will feature on your Cornish travels, whether it's fresh crab from the Fern Pit Café and Ferry – which you'll come across on this walk – fish and chips on the beach in Newquay, a slice of stargazy pie in Mousehole or a more sophisticated seafood dish in one of Rick Stein's Padstow restaurants. If you time your trip right, oysters might even be on the menu – the boisterous Falmouth Oyster Festival celebrates this much-loved delicacy when the Fal Estuary's oyster-dredging season gets going in October.

But it's Cornwall's other historic industry, mining, that we have to thank for the pasty – that quick and easy pocket-sized picnic beloved by locals and holidaymakers in equal measure. Although there's some debate about the origins of these delicious all-in-one meals, it's widely believed that their chunky crusts functioned as handholds for mucky-fingered miners, to be discarded at the end of their meal. Traditionally, pasties are filled with beef, swede, onions and a smattering of pepper, although nowadays there are all kinds of fillings, including cheese and onion, pork and apple, lamb and mint, roasted vegetables, and even mackerel and horseradish. Pasties can be bought all over the county, in pubs, cafés and at beachside stalls.

In a similar way, there's no shortage of establishments offering that sacred West Country afternoon rite – the cream tea. The Cosy Nook Tea Gardens and Restaurant, a suggested stop on this walk, is one such place, its home-baked scones served with sticky homemade jam and lashings of local clotted cream (remember: jam goes first in Cornwall, always). And it's the very same rich, creamy milk used to make this clotted cream that goes into the county's outstanding fudge, ice creams and 60-plus varieties of cheese. Of these, Cornish Yarg, a semi-hard cow's-milk cheese wrapped in a coating of edible nettle leaves, and the multi-award-winning Cornish Blue, are probably the best known.

07 Dodman Point and Gorran Haven

A journey through time

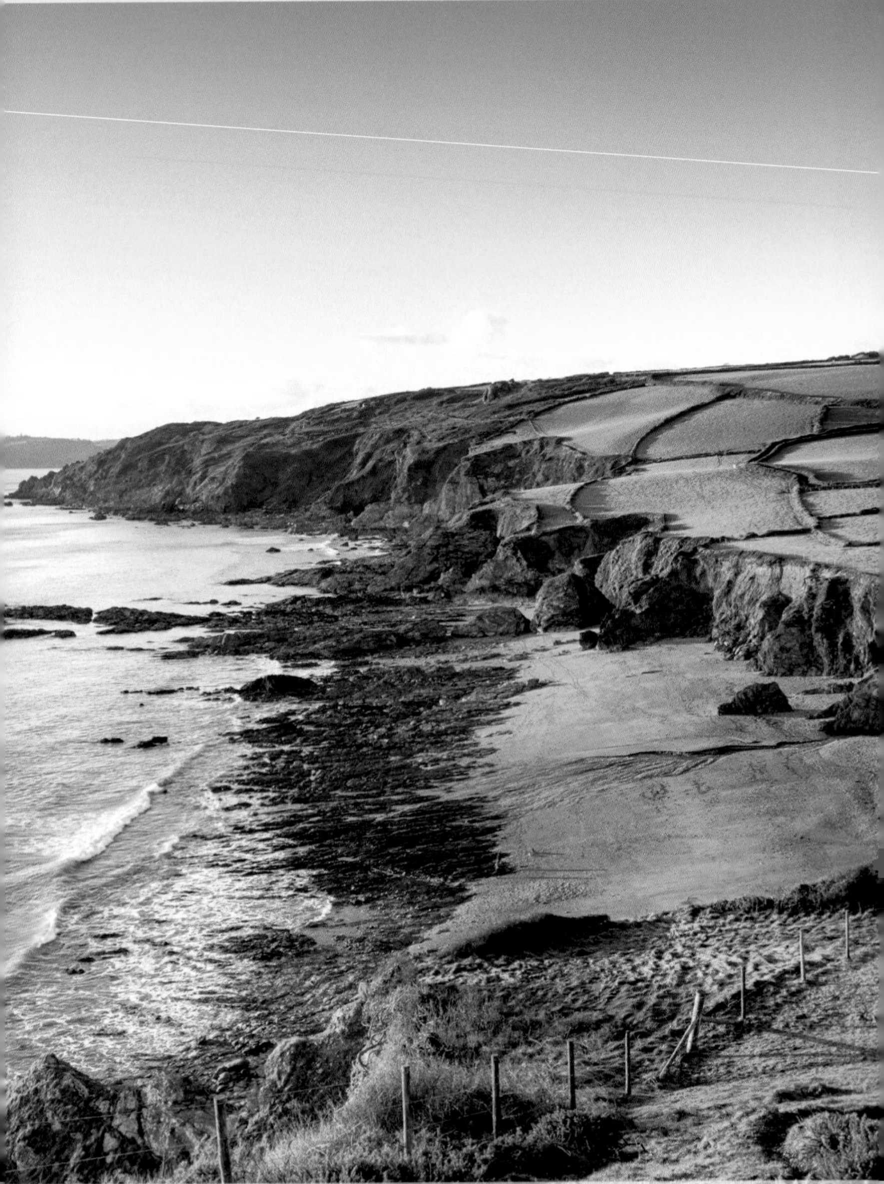

170m | 286m | E | 8km | 2hrs | -4.5km

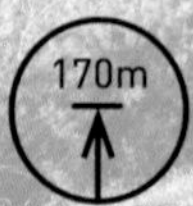

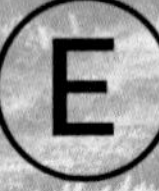

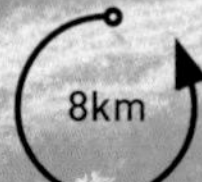

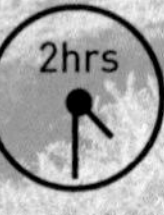

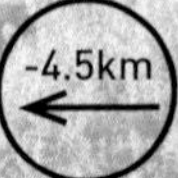

07

Beautiful scenery and atmospheric historical sites punctuate this peaceful walk, which is a breath of fresh air after the busy tourist towns of the south coast. Stop off at one of the quiet sandy beaches along the way for a swim or a picnic, ensuring you allow enough time to explore the unspoilt fishing village of Gorran Haven afterwards. Here, from the harbour wall, you can see fish darting about in the crystal-clear water below. If you skip the option for a picnic at Vault Beach earlier in the route, this cute seaside community is the ideal place for a cuppa or a sandwich before continuing on your journey inland, along picturesque country lanes back to the start.

07 Dodman Point and Gorran Haven

A journey through time

CLIMBS

GETTING THERE

This walk starts at the Dodman Point National Trust car park at Penare (£2 suggested donation), to the southwest of Gorran Haven. PL26 6NY will take you to a holiday park, but keep going and you will soon arrive in Penare.

NOTE: Try to avoid driving through Mevagissey on the way to Gorran Haven, as the narrow and winding one-way system can get very congested.

WALK DIRECTIONS

1. Exit the car park at the far end, cross the road, go up the steps, through the gate and walk downhill with the fence on your right. Soon, the secluded Hemmick Beach can be seen and accessed downhill to the right, but to continue the route, fork left, downhill at first, then uphill on the coast path (the sea will be on your right). Now simply follow the main coast path until you reach the stone cross of Dodman Point.

2. The large granite cross at Dodman Point – the highest headland on the south Cornish coast – was erected in 1896 as a navigational aid for sailors. At the cross, turn onto the small path leading inland through a small field. You will pass the National Trust-owned Watch House, an 18th-century building that was erected as part of a chain of coastal signal stations designed to thwart a Napoleonic invasion. After the Watch House, look for the remains of the hillfort on your left.

NOT TO MISS

Iron Age hillfort

A vast Iron Age hillfort (SX002396) once dominated Dodman Point. Its walls can still be seen from high ground today. The structure, which is hundreds of metres long, is around 2,000 years old and has a secondary defensive structure in the form of a large bulwark, which runs across the whole headland – see map.

3. Continue past the fort and across the field on the path then, as you near the far end of the field, veer left and rejoin the coast path. You should reach a junction – fork right towards Vault beach, a great spot for a picnic.

SHORTCUT – This is a handy shortcut which shortens the route to about 3.5km. In Instruction 3, fork left at the junction for Vault Beach and walk to a track. Turn right and follow between fields back to Penare.

4 Now the route takes you along a pretty section past Vault beach (take a lower pathway to the right if you want to go down onto the sand). The coast path will eventually lead you around the headland to Gorran Haven, where you'll find two small but perfectly formed beaches with beautifully clear water. As you enter the village, ignore the first left turn, but turn left at the second uphill, past the shops and cafés.

5 You will pass the Cakebread Bakery (see opposite) on your right, a public convenience on your left and then a car park on your right. After the car park, bear right when you meet the junction with Lamledra Hill.

NOT TO MISS

Gorran Haven

This small, unspoilt fishing village has an ancient harbour. The first recorded use of long nets to catch pilchards in the county took place here in 1270.

6 Roughly 200m further up the lane, turn left onto the small access road, following the public-footpath sign – note Corner Cottage on your right. Go right at the houses at the end, then through the gate onto the path. After a further 100m or so, go over the stepping stones, through another gate, and follow all the way to Treveague Farm. Here, go right onto the small road then, after a few metres, left and through the campsite.

7 On the far side of the campsite, go through the gate and straight up the track between the fields. After the next gate, join the road straight ahead and walk down the hill. Follow this road back to Penare and the car park where you started the walk.

THE PITSTOPS

Cakebread Bakery

Shop, bakery, café and post office rolled into one, the Cakebread Bakery is at the heart of the community. Expect homemade dishes, including cream teas and delicious pasties, and local beers.
Canton, Gorran Haven, St Austell PL26 6JG. Open daily
01726 842048

Mermaid Cafe

This classic British seaside café has a distinctly Cornish twist, with the obligatory mug of tea and hot Cornish pasty on the chalkboard. Open rain or shine every day in the season, and situated just over half way round our walk, it's the ideal pitstop.
The beach, Gorran Haven. Open from the week before Easter to the end of September daily.

THE EXTRA STEP

Painting in Cornwall

Cornish art can be neatly divided between the north and south coasts, between Modernists and Naturalists, between St Ives – with its outpost of the Tate Gallery above Porthmeor Beach – and the Penlee House Gallery and Museum in Penzance, with its collection of historic local works.

In the early years of the 19th century, European travel opportunities were scarce due to the Napoleonic Wars, during which naval ships posed a danger to passenger vessels. This led to domestic tourism and the British Grand Tour, a local alternative to the better-known Grand Tour of Europe, which had become a cultural rite of passage for young men from the nobility and wealthy landed gentry. In 1811, JMW Turner was commissioned to produce a series of images depicting the coasts of Devon and Cornwall. Captivated by their dramatic seas, storms and shipwrecks, he produced a large number of paintings and sketches that were reproduced for the pages of an early guidebook, designed to bring sightseers to the region. His contemporary William Daniell went on a similar mission, producing countless watercolours of the British coastline, many of which were inspired by the West Country, including Gorran Haven.

Over the following decades, just as French painters packed their easels and headed for Brittany, so English painters headed for their own Celtic outpost, Cornwall. The Royal Academician Stanhope Forbes settled in the fishing village of Newlyn in 1884, where he founded the Newlyn School in 1899. It soon became a vibrant community of 20 or so artists, who spent much of their time mingling with the fishing community in and around Newlyn Harbour. Forbes's 1885 painting *Fish Sale on a Cornish Beach* became emblematic of the group's desire to paint *en plein air* – that is, out in the open air – evoking the spirit of Cornwall through an emphasis on social realism and the everyday lives of its working people. The Penlee Gallery in Penzance, which occupies a fine 1895 building that was financed by the Cornish entrepreneur and philanthropist John Passmore Edwards, is the best place for an overview of this spellbinding body of work.

Initially drawn to the area by the Newlyn School, Samuel John Birch settled a few kilometres further south, at Lamorna Cove, in 1892. In his adopted home, the artist (affectionately nicknamed 'Lamorna' Birch by Forbes) established a new circle of artists, which included Laura and Harold Knight, in 1907. As part of this group, Laura Knight painted *The Beach* in 1908, which depicts children playing in rock pools in bright sunlight. Years later, she wrote of Cornwall: 'Nostalgia comes each spring in London, for the rain, for the mist, for the mud and dung, for thick shoes and a mackintosh, for the glory that is Cornwall, the mystic Cornwall that goes to people's heads and makes them a little queer.'

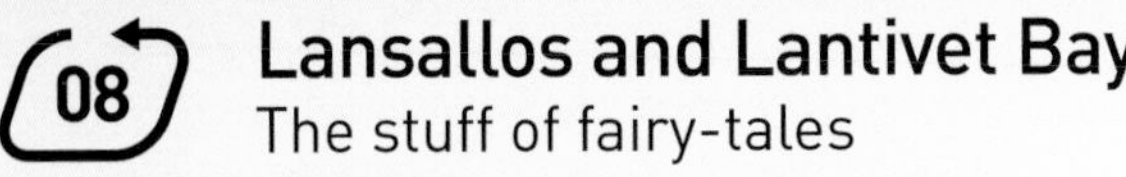

Lansallos and Lantivet Bay

The stuff of fairy-tales

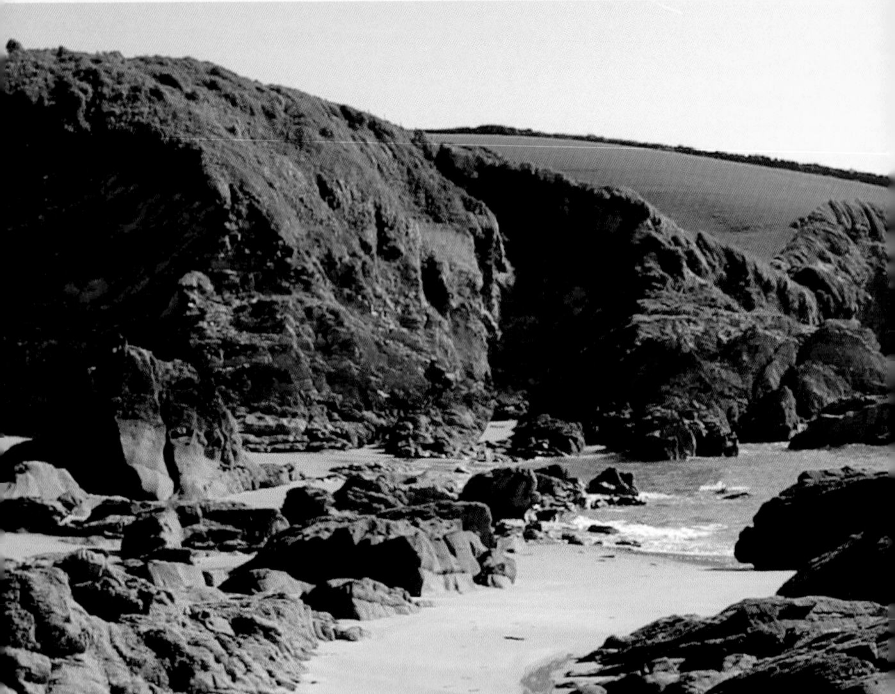

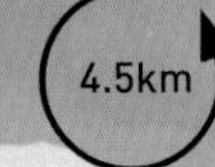

This circuit is full of variety, especially when you consider its moderate length. It runs down leafy lanes, across open fields, through woodland, across streams and down to a beautiful sandy beach. Wander around the grounds of the church of St Ildierna, in the historic village of Lansallos, before heading to Lantivet Bay, where you'll find pretty Lansallos Cove and the evocatively named Frog Prince Cove – a wonderfully secluded little beach that remains unmarked on any map or chart. As the tide goes out here, a stretch of fine sand emerges and the clear water beckons bathers. A walk for all weathers, this route is ruggedly beautiful on stormy days, still pretty on grey days and has jaw-dropping appeal on sunny days, when you'll want to do it all over again!

08 Lansallos and Lantivet Bay

The stuff of fairy-tales

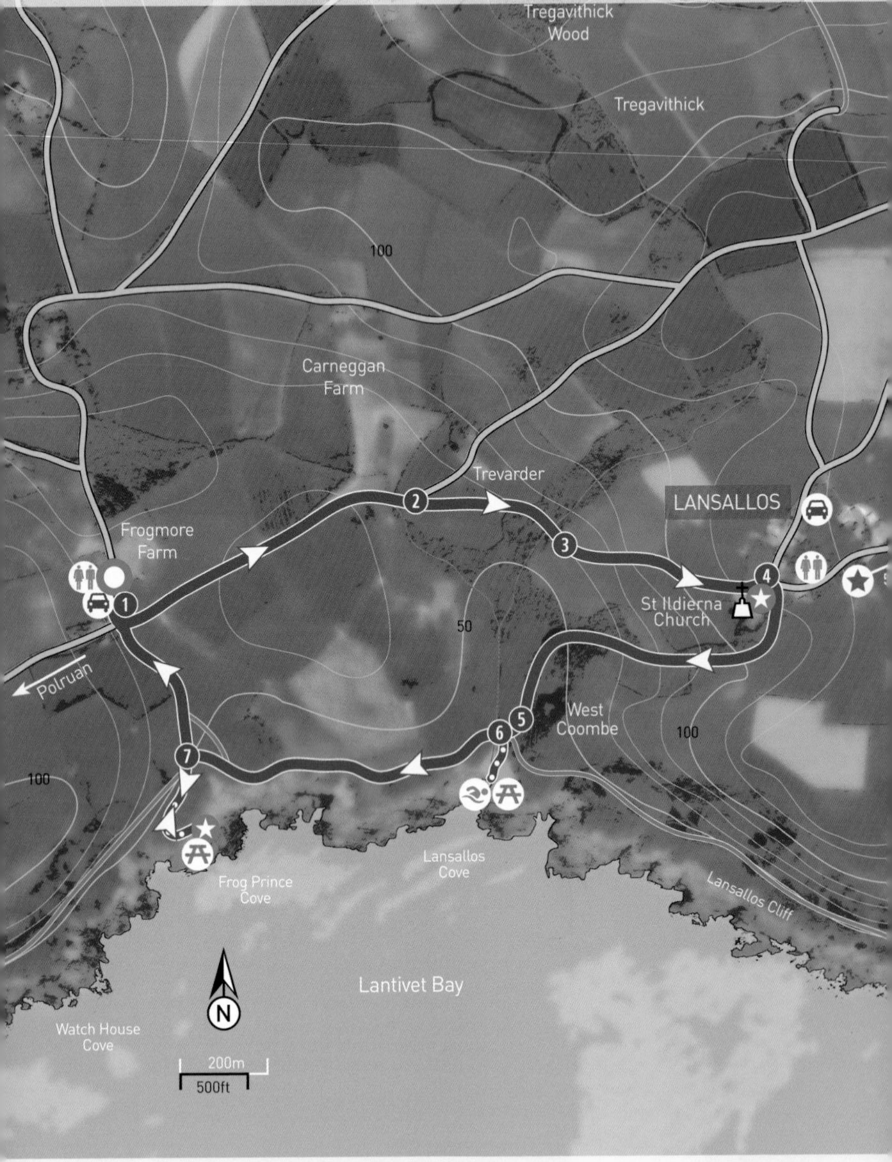

Landlawren
Tregavithick Wood
Tregavithick
100
Carneggan Farm
Trevarder
LANSALLOS
Frogmore Farm
St Ildierna Church
50
Polruan
West Coombe
100
100
Lansallos Cove
Frog Prince Cove
Lansallos Cliff
Lantivet Bay
N
Watch House Cove
200m
500ft

CLIMBS

175m
150m
125m
100m
75m
50m
0.5km
1.0km
3km
1.5km
2.0km
2.5km
3.0km
3.5km
4.0km
4.5km

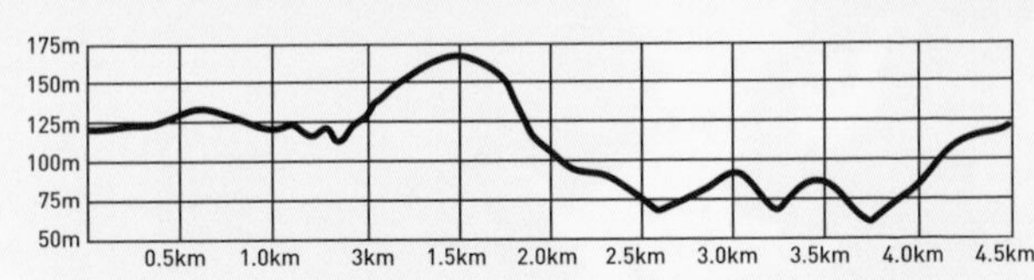

GETTING THERE

The start point is quite hard to find – about 2 miles east of Polruan. Using a sat nav, the postcode will take you to Frogmore Farm. The car park and start point is just opposite the farm. PL23 1NP.

WALK DIRECTIONS

1. Go through the gate opposite the entrance to the car park and walk 100m or so to the lane and then turn left. Here, striking hedgerows support many species of birds and insects, including beautiful butterflies and dragonflies.

2. Keep to the lane for about 1km and, just after a stream, go up the steps on the right-hand side of the road. Follow the path across the field towards the church tower of St Ildierna church (see p.86) on the far horizon. Go through the gate into the woods, downhill on the path, over the bridge and uphill a few metres to a path junction.

3. Go left at the junction and out of the woods. Go through two gates. Then, in the field, follow the left-hand border and, in the next field, walk directly towards the church. Go over the stone steps (traversing a wall) onto the grassy path next to the church and, after 100m, you reach an asphalt lane.

4. At the asphalt lane, turn directly to your right onto the smaller lane (almost a track) and follow this for 100m to join the path on the left. This will lead you all the way down, roughly 1.5km, to Lansallos Cove. (Don't turn off where you see the bridge.)

5. Near the coast, after the first gate, go straight ahead through the second gate then fork right. This will take you down to a junction with the coast path. Here, you can go straight ahead to the beach.

6. To continue, turn right instead of straight ahead to the beach. Walk up the steep hill to a field. Keep going on the path until you reach a third field. Here, walk along the path closest to the coast, down into the valley and up the other side. At the top, follow the left-hand fence line and let it lead you around the back of a small sea inlet to a bench.

OPTIONAL EXTRA – To visit Frog Prince Cove, walk past the bench and join the path through the bushes. Go left when you reach the junction and follow your nose down to the sand. (Veer left when you are nearly at the bottom to access the best part of the beach.)

NOT TO MISS

St Ildierna church

This ancient church was dedicated in 1321 and has since been extensively renovated and extended. Inside, there are a number of significant features, including a carved wagon roof, a Norman font and oak pews that date from between 1490 and 1520. The church has a peal of eight bells and a team of dedicated bell-ringers, known for its success in competitions.

7 To finish the route, from the bench, follow the path to the right, uphill, and directly inland. You will quickly merge with a more defined path and be heading towards the trees. You will meet two gates; go through the smaller gate on the right and onto the pathway that takes you between fields to a lane. Opposite where you join the lane is a gate; go through this and you are on the path you took from opposite the car park earlier. Follow through and back to the start point.

NOT TO MISS

Frog Prince Cove

The very definition of a secret beach, Frog Prince Cove is a tiny, secluded strip of sand that remains unmarked on any map or chart. So secret is this cove, in fact, that we've coined our own name for it, Frog Prince Cove, which encompasses its fairy-tale ambience, its proximity to the hamlet of Frogmore and the amphibian-shaped rock that stands nearby. But it's not just the beach that's worth exploring here – the clear waters around it are, too. Just a 100m splash away, past plenty of smooth-sand resting places and jump-perfect rocks, lies adjacent Palace Cove – one of many miniature beaches in this small area, which must be one of the best wild-swimming spots in Cornwall. When water levels rise, only the small area of sand next to the beach-access path at Frog Prince Cove remains accessible, but if you swim to the left, you'll find more dry sand in a larger inlet. Frog Prince Cove also features in our sister publication *Secret Beaches: Southwest England*.

THE PITSTOP

Blue Peter Inn

This much-loved harbourside inn offers fabulous food, real ales, lagers and local scrumpy, as well as live music and a roaring fire. Quay Road, Polperro, Looe PL13 2QZ. Open daily. 01503 272743 www.thebluepeterinn.yolasite.com

THE EXTRA STEP

Daphne du Maurier in Fowey

The English author Daphne du Maurier lived for nearly 30 years in and around the small south-coast port of Fowey, just a few kilometres from this walk, and found inspiration for much of her writing in the county (see also p.116). She first visited Cornwall on holiday with her parents, who were so taken with the Fowey estuary that they bought a cottage there in 1927, when Daphne had just turned 20. The young writer penned her first novel, *The Loving Spirit* (1931), soon after this. Over her three decades in the area, Du Maurier lived in several different houses, including the Georgian grey-stone mansion Menabilly, just west of Fowey, which became the inspiration for Manderlay, the house in her most famous novel, *Rebecca* (1938).

Further down the coast, the muddy, wooded inlets of the Helford River form the backdrop to Du Maurier's *Frenchman's Creek* (1941), a novel set during the reign of King Charles II. The story chronicles the love affair between an impulsive Englishwoman who goes to Cornwall to escape her suffocating high-society London life and a notorious French pirate she finds hiding out there. The fiction of a French privateer anchored in a Cornish creek, unsuspected by local people, seems, at first, unlikely – that is, until you visit the south bank of the Helford River, where thick undergrowth and densely matted branches overhead afford only the occasional glimpse of the water, mud banks and wading seabirds. It's better, by far, to view it from one of the pleasure boats that sets out daily from Falmouth.

Du Maurier's final novel, *Rule Britannia* (1972), is a funny yet chilling futuristic fantasy about Cornwall. Set in an imagined financial crisis, Britain is bailed out by the United States, upon which it becomes dependent. That is, until the Cornish launch their own successful rearguard action in an attempt to protect their heritage and traditions in the face of this military occupation. It's a tribute to the place that Du Maurier adored and that took her to its heart, as was her lesser-known non-fiction title, *Vanishing Cornwall* (1967), which includes photographs by her son, Christian Browning. Today, Fowey hosts an annual Du Maurier Festival, a week-long arts event in memory of the writer who made her home here and who famously declared: 'Fowey has a magic all of its own'.

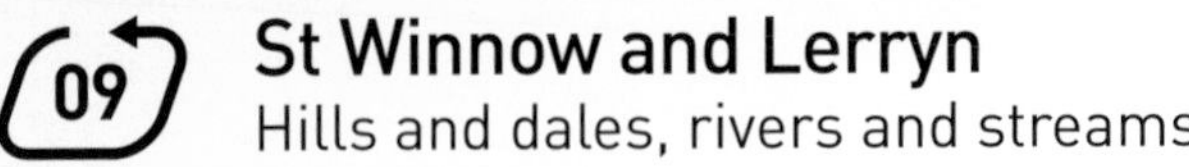

09 St Winnow and Lerryn

Hills and dales, rivers and streams

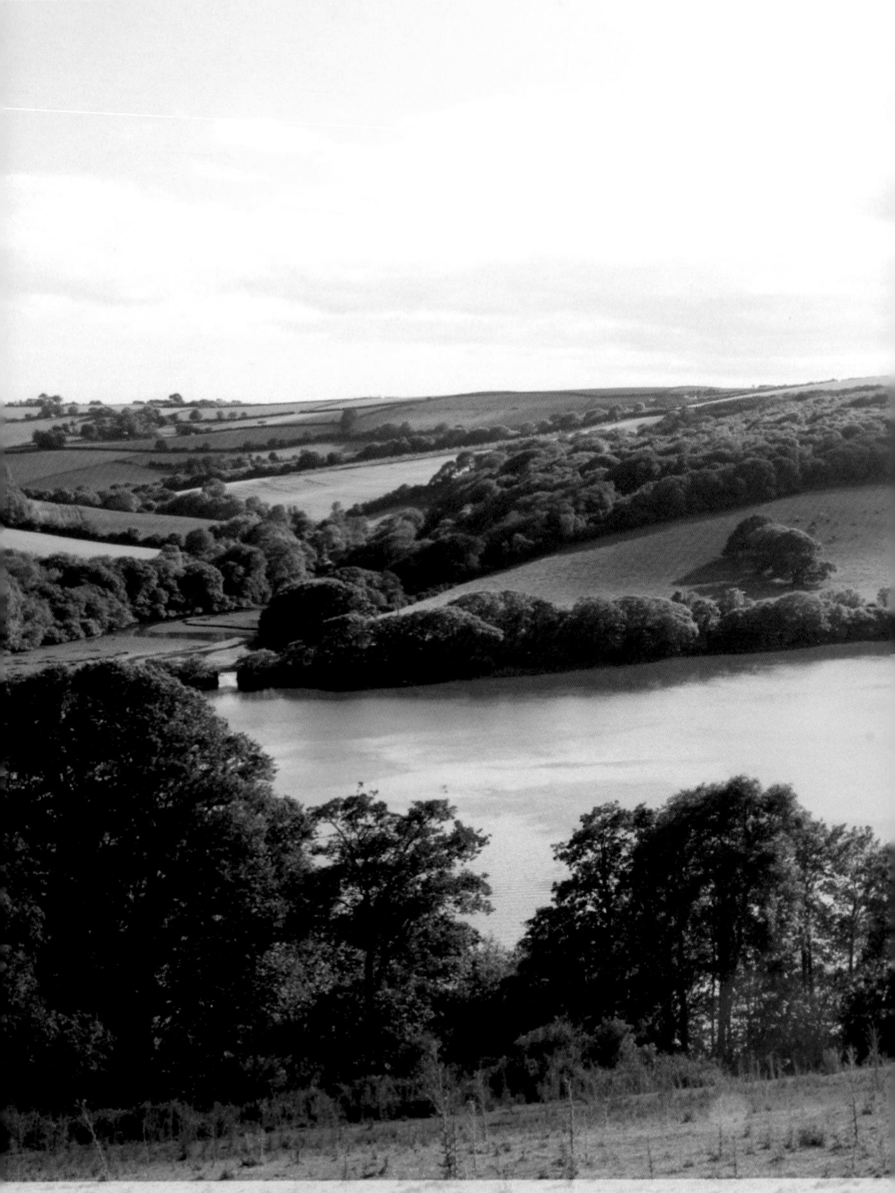

134m | 250m | E/M | 7.5km | 2.5hrs | +0.5km | -2km

You'll see some of Cornwall's prettiest inland scenery on this route, which takes in hills, fields, and the banks and tributaries of the tidal rivers Lerryn and Fowey. Expect easy-to-follow paths, peaceful picnic spots and some well-placed Pitstops along the way. You'll pass through the former smuggling stronghold of Lerryn (Brandy Lane in the village is the giveaway!) and past National Trust Ethy wood. Please note: there are often cows in the fields, and they can get anxious around dogs, particularly if they have calves in tow, so it's important to keep hounds on leads at all times.

09 St Winnow and Lerryn

Hills and dales, rivers and streams

Grenville Road
LOSTWITHIEL
Two Trees Road
Lanwithan Road
Newham Lane
Trewether
Tredethick
Redlake Cottage Meadows Nature Reserve
Redlake Cottage
Tawell Farm
Colwood Wood
N
400m
1,000ft
Newham
Tregays
St Winnow Mill
Ethy
Lerryn
Collon
Church Park
River Lerryn
St Winnow
Lantyan Wood
Ethy Wood
Mill Wood
Middle Wood
Ten Acre Wood
Lerryn Wood
West Wood
Great Wood
Manley Wood
River Fowey
Woodgate Wood
Brighton Wood
Manely
Wringford
St Veep
River Fowey
Water Lane
Golant

CLIMBS

130m
110m
90m
70m
50m
1km 2km 3km 4km 5km 6km 7km 8km

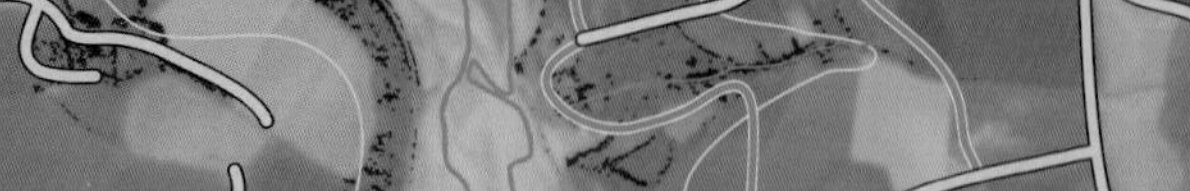

GETTING THERE

Take Lanwithan Road south out of Lostwithiel. After about a mile, you'll see a right turn in the direction of St Winnow (this is the first sign for St Winnow that you'll see). Drive down it for just over a mile and park near the church, museum or Angie's Cream Teas – the first of our Pitstops. PL22 0LF.

NOT TO MISS

St Winnow church

The bulk of this riverside church dates back to the 15th century, although parts, including traces of stonework on the northern side, survive from Norman times. Many updates have ensued throughout the centuries, including a 19th-century restoration. The church is noted for its magnificent stained-glass windows.

WALK DIRECTIONS

1. Take the footpath to the right of Angie's Cream Teas (see p.97), go through two gates and after 250m, where the track bends to the left, go over the stile and into the field. Now views begin to open up of the surrounding countryside and you will be following yellow arrows through fields, but you'll need the following instructions as well: walk diagonally right across this first field, then go over the double stile into the next field and follow the left-hand border.

2. In the next field, go diagonally across to the right, towards a gate. Go into the next field and walk to the far bottom-left corner. After another stile, follow the left-hand hedge and go over a stile about halfway along. Walk down the steep field near the right-hand border and you pass a house on the right. Just after the house, go over the stile to the lane.

3. Turn right to walk along the lane, then fork left into the National Trust property of Ethy. Follow into the dip and then, where the track reaches the top of a rise, turn left onto the path heading uphill.

SHORTCUT – Knocking about 2km off the route, this shortcut removes the final section to Lerryn across fields and back along the estuary. In Instruction 3, instead of turning left onto the pathway at the top of the rise, keep going on the track all the way through Ethy Wood until you reach the Lerryn estuary. You rejoin the route in Instruction 6, where the estuary path follows around the creek, near the picnic spot. You will need to turn right over the bridge to be back on the route.

4. On the path heading uphill, fork left at two subsequent junctions and you will find yourself at a small gate to exit the woods. Walk directly across the field, passing under the boughs of the large tree. Go into the next field at the opening and bear left to go through a gate after a few metres. Now follow the left-hand field border for about 100m, after which you carry on across the field on the same bearing. You are heading for a gate to the right of the houses.

5. When you emerge onto the residential street from the field, go left, walk to the T-junction and then turn right down to the River Lerryn. Here, if the tide is low, you have an optional extra to go across the stepping stones to the two Pitstops (see opposite). (There is also a bridge.)

6. To continue the route, before crossing the stepping stones, walk along the lane with the estuary on your left. The lane gets narrower and eventually turns into a path. After about 1.5km along the estuary, the path turns inland. Note the pretty picnic spot just here, and then go around the back of a creek – be sure to turn left and go over the small bridge to keep following the estuary. (This is where the shortcut joins.)

7. Soon you will reach a wide track. Turn left here, then, after 200m or so, turn left onto a small path. Follow along to the stream, cross over and keep left to stay by the river. After a couple of hundred metres more, you will rejoin the wide track from before; go left again.

8. Where the track bends to the right there is a bench. Take a moment to admire the estuary view here. Now you are on the bank of the River Fowey; keep following the wide track. After about 1.5km, the track turns into a woodland path and eventually you reach a field. Follow the left-hand border to the small bridge.

9. After the bridge, you will find yourself at the water's edge. Here on the grassy area is our second picnic spot. Where you see the wooden post, you can either walk to the right onto the path inland (high-tide route) and then follow easily back through the field to the start point; or you can walk along the estuary edge (low-tide route), past the church and to the quay, where you can head up the track to the start.

THE PITSTOPS

Angie's Cream Teas

Located by the church in St Winnow, this cute caravan is a great place to fuel up before or after your walk. Refreshments include cream teas, home-baked cakes and superb local sausages.
St Winnow, Lostwithiel PL22 0LF. Open Apr–Oct daily. 01208 873742

Lerryn River Stores

The shop in the heart of Lerryn has everything you might need for a picnic lunch, from local cider, cheese and award-winning meats to ready-made sandwiches, pasties and cream teas. Grab a treat to enjoy on the picnic benches down by the river.
Fore Street, Lerryn, Lostwithiel PL22 0PT. Open daily (reduced hours in winter). 01208 872375. www.lerrynriver.co.uk

The Ship Inn

Part pub, part local library, this is the perfect place to come for a pint, a good read and some fine pub grub. Eat in the bar, restaurant or garden and expect locally sourced meat, fish and vegetables.
Fore Street, Lerryn, Lostwithiel PL22 0PT. Open daily
01208 872374. www.theshipinnlerryn.co.uk

THE EXTRA STEP

The castles and country houses of Cornwall

Cornwall is famous for its evocative ruins and fine stately homes and gardens, which bring to life so many of the people, places and events that shaped the county in days gone by. Two such historic sites, Restormel Castle and Lanhydrock House, lie very close to this walk, just above the River Fowey between Lostwithiel and Bodmin; the rest are scattered around the county.

English Heritage maintains most of Cornwall's castles, including the best known of them all, Tintagel, that magnificent and moody north-coast bastion so famously associated with the legends of King Arthur. Although there's no historical evidence to support this connection, there's no better place in Britain to immerse yourself in the tales of courtly love and dastardly betrayals that inhabit the legends of King Arthur, Camelot, the Holy Grail and, of course, the love triangle between Arthur, Guinevere and Lancelot.

Tintagel is one of the county's main Norman castles, as is Restormel, which is situated on a high spur above the River Fowey. This perfectly circular structure is spectacular at any time of year, but particularly in the spring, when the grounds are covered in a stunning carpet of bluebells. In 1999, Cornish nationalists removed English Heritage signs at Restormel, claiming that the striking building was part of Cornish heritage along with the Cornish language, the kilt and bagpipes, their native bird – the Cornish chough – and their patron saint, St Piran. Further west along the south coast lies Pendennis, perched on the west bank of the mouth of the River Fal, and St Mawes, its opposite number on the east bank, which were built by Henry VIII to protect the great natural harbour at Falmouth.

When you've had your fill of ruins, head for one of the county's beautifully preserved country houses, most of which are owned by the National Trust. Tudor-built Cotehele (see also p.106), in the parish of Calstock near Cornwall's eastern border, is one of the least altered of its kind, while nearby Antony is a superb 18th-century stone mansion that tells the extraordinary story of a family caught up in events of the English Civil War. Just a stone's throw from this route and an easy walk from Bodmin Parkway station, Lanhydrock is an excellent example of a great Victorian house and grounds. For centuries, this fine building was home to the same family, who endured a devastating fire and then tragedy during World War I. Events are put on at Lanhydrock throughout the year, including open-air theatre productions, garden tours and a variety of children's activities.

Further down the coast, beyond Falmouth, lie Trebah Garden, which is run as a charitable trust, and National Trust-owned Glendurgan Garden, with its sloping laurel maze that confounds and amuses visitors. Both of these magnificent gardens run down through sloping sub-tropical vegetation, where jungles of giant rhubarb plants lead down to the pretty south-facing swimming beaches of the Helford River.

Just as important to walkers as these historic estates is the National Trust's role in protecting and preserving large swathes of unspoilt, yet ever-changing, coastline. Trust members get free use of more than 40 car parks across the county, often in quite remote spots, which can be invaluable for walkers wanting to access the wildest parts of the county.

10 Cadson Bury Hill

Prehistory, paddling and plants

156m | 140m | E | 2.5km | 1hr | -1.5km

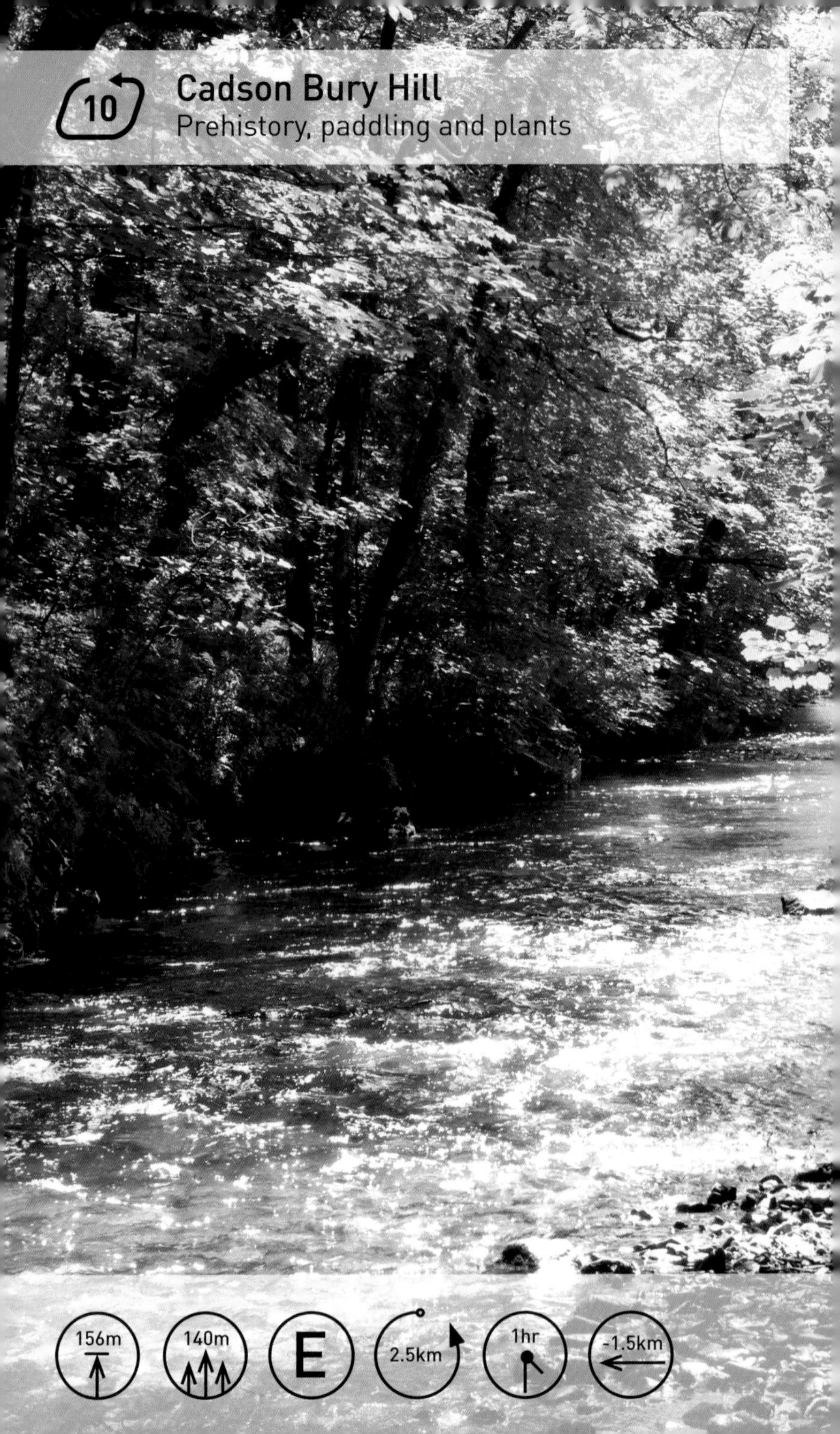

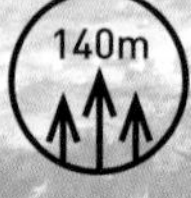

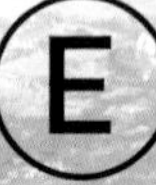

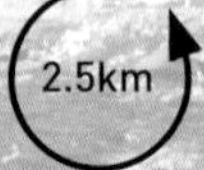

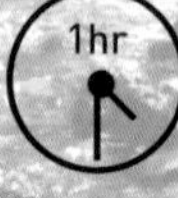

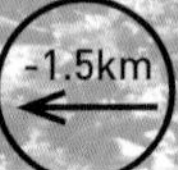

This route includes two starkly contrasting sections – a challenging uphill stretch followed by a leisurely riverside stroll. After the initial climb up through ancient woodland, you'll come to the hillfort of Cadson Bury, an important relic of Cornwall's Iron Age landscape, from where there are sweeping valley views. Beyond this, down by the River Lynher, you'll come to points in the river that are deep enough for swimming, as well as excellent paddling spots. For anyone who wants to stay dry, the riverbanks are the perfect place from which to launch skimming stones, pick wild raspberries, spot kingfishers or simply spread a blanket and relax. For families with very young children, the route can be shortened to only about 1km and still take in a pretty section of riverbank.

10 Cadson Bury Hill

Prehistory, paddling and plants

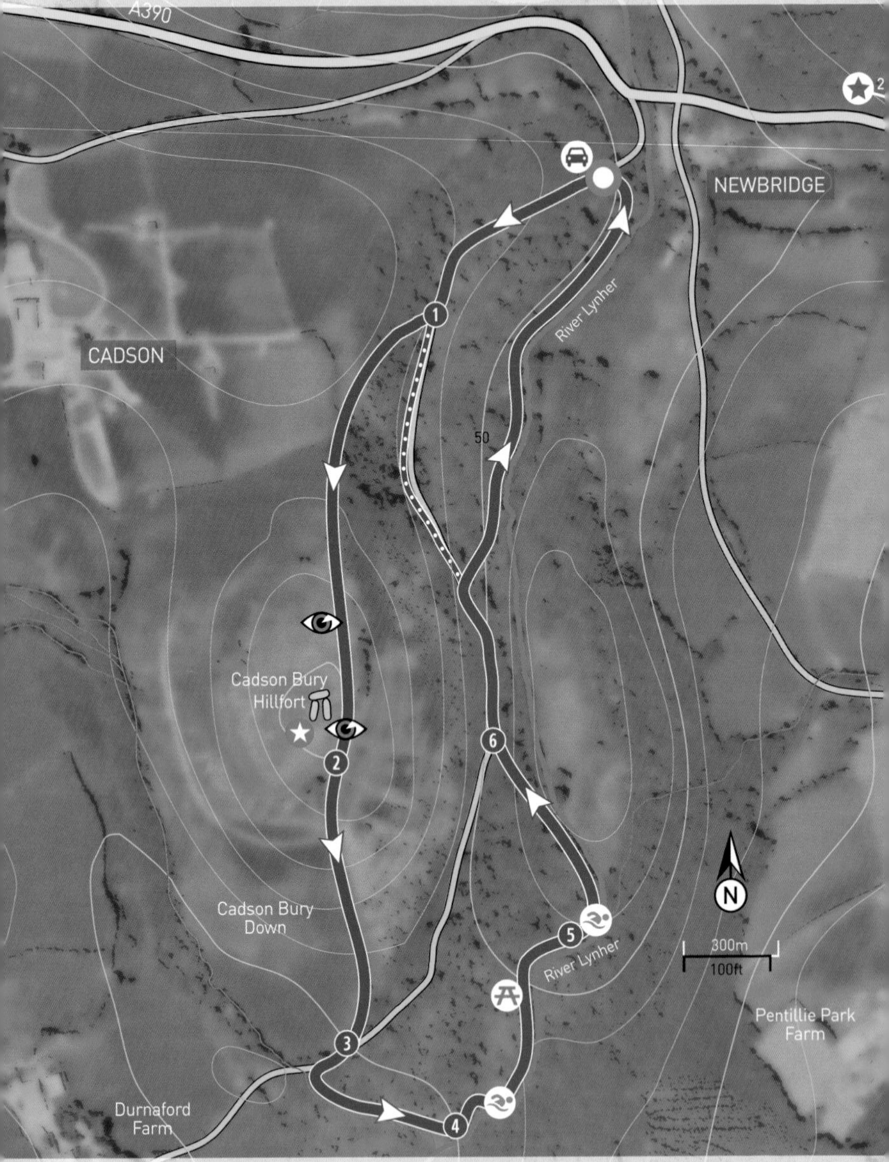

50
The Mill
A390
NEWBRIDGE
CADSON
River Lynher
50
Cadson Bury Hillfort
Cadson Bury Down
Durnaford Farm
River Lynher
Pentillie Park Farm
N
300m
100ft
1
2
3
4
5
6
Park Wood

CLIMBS

160m
140m
120m
100m
80m
0.25km
0.50km
0.75km
1.00km
1.25km
1.50km
1.75km
2.00km
2.25km
2.50km

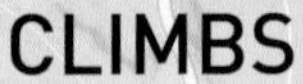

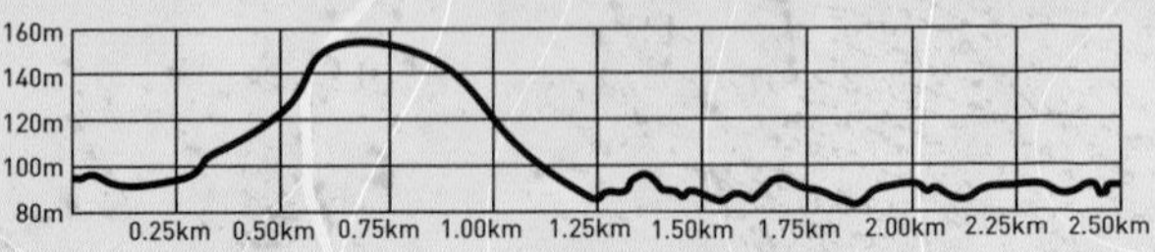

GETTING THERE

The start point for this route is in Newbridge, a small village on the A390 near Callington, to the east of Liskeard. The best way to reach it is to leave Callington on the A390 in the direction of Liskeard. When you arrive in Newbridge, cross over the small bridge and turn immediately left onto a small lane. A car park can be found a little way down on the left. PL17 7HL.

WALK DIRECTIONS

1. Walk down the lane, away from the A390 and, after about 250m, turn onto the path on your right. Walk uphill (for the most part) on this woodland trail. You will go over a stile near the top, after which the path opens up at the top of the hill to incredible views.

SHORTCUT – To shorten the route to a 1km loop, simply keep walking along the lane until you see the gates on your left. Join the riverside pathway and walk back the 500m to the parking area.

2. The path around the hillfort forks both right and left. Take the left path to the fort entrance, denoted by a post with a red dot. But be sure to have a walk around the area here – the views are spectacular – before returning to the post to head down the hill. After a few metres, the path veers right; just here, look for the ditch, a final barricade of the fort. After about 150m and a gate, walk down the left-hand side of the field.

3. Go through the kissing gate and turn right onto the lane. Then, after about 50m, turn left onto the path and walk alongside the stream.

4. When you reach the River Lynher, turn left onto the wide path. The boggy ground on the river's bank supports a number of grasses, deciduous plants and perennials, and the mud here can preserve animal tracks for quite a while, so keep your eyes peeled for otter prints.

5. Alongside the river there are some lovely picnic areas – explore some of the small paths leading off from the main track. After a few hundred metres, you'll come across a deep river pool. When the water is not flowing too fast here, it's an ideal spot for swimming.

6. Keep going alongside the river. At one point, you will join a lane but then rejoin the riverside pathway for the final 500m or so. You will eventually see the car park where you started, behind the trees on your left.

NOT TO MISS

Cadson Bury hillfort

This ancient hillfort was established in the 3rd and 4th centuries BC. Little remains of the original structure, except a single rampart that closely follows the hilltop contours, and entrances that are clearly visible from the summit. The fort is thought to have been used for ceremonies rather than settlement, as people tended to live down by the river – though, in times of warfare, these people would have sought refuge in the fort. It would also have been a hub of trade and communal activity. In the 18th century, this became one of the most important mining areas in the country, with deposits of silver found in nearby Silver Valley. (SX343673)

THE PITSTOPS

The Carpenter's Arms

This historic, family-run pub, which is located about 10km to the east of this walk, serves delicious, locally sourced food. It's named after the carpenters who built nearby Cotehele House (see p.106).
Lower Metherell, Callington PL17 8BJ. Open Mon–Thu 2–midnight, Fri–Sat midday–1, Sun midday–midnight. 01579 351148

Louis Tea Rooms

Expect cream teas, delicious meals and panoramic views of the Tamar Valley. There's also an on-site farm shop.
Kit Hill Approach Road, Kit Hill, Callington PL17 8AX. Open Mon–Sat 9–8, Sun 9–5. 01579 389223. www.louistearooms.weebly.com

THE EXTRA STEP

Cornwall's coastal railways

Cornwall is home to some of the most scenic railway lines in Britain. Passing through rolling fields and wooded valleys, historic villages and market towns, over and under viaducts, and alongside beautiful estuaries and stretches of coast, these branch lines were built in the second half of the 19th century to transport tin, copper, fruit and vegetables away from the remotest parts of the county on the first leg of their journey to Plymouth, London and beyond. One of the most popular of these, known today as the Tamar Valley Line, lies just a few kilometres east of this walk.

This historic line runs north from Plymouth in Devon to the Cornish village of Gunnislake, skirting the River Tamar for much of its journey. The highlight of the route is the Calstock Viaduct, a towering construction that straddles the river between the villages of Bere Alston and Calstock. Built between 1904 and 1907, this giant arched bridge is 37m high and made from a staggering 11,148 blocks of concrete. From the top, you'll be able to catch glimpses of National Trust-owned Cotehele House and Gardens (see also p.99), nestled in the woods below, which is accessible via a gentle riverside walk.

Walk in the other direction along the river from the viaduct, and you'll come to the historic river port of Morwellham Quay. Now an open-air museum comprising a restored Victorian village, a farm, the Charlotte copper mine and a port – complete with docks and quays – this ancient settlement, which occupies a strategic position at the centre of the Tamar Valley, was developed to support the local mining industry. However, its role was thwarted with the coming of the railways, which made the export of minerals more efficient than ever before. Morwellham Quay provided the backdrop for the 2010–2011 BBC television series *Edwardian Farm*.

Back on the Tamar Valley Line, expect a quirky manoeuvre at Bere Alston, where the train must reverse due to an awkward arrangement of tracks – a legacy of the station's early years as a railway junction. It's a similar story on the Looe Valley Line, a little way down the coast, which sees the train come to a complete standstill in a field at Coombe, where the driver must swap ends before the journey can continue. Just a couple of the fittingly eccentric features you can expect on some of the region's oldest stretches of railway.

Further west, other branch lines include the Atlantic Coast line, which links Par to Newquay through china-clay country, with its 19th-century industrial remains; the Maritime Line, which runs from Truro to Falmouth, connecting the port to London; and the St Ives Bay Line, which links St Erth to St Ives and is by far the best way to arrive in the town, sweeping along the golden fringes of the bay. Anyone planning a trip on a Cornish branch line might like to turn it into a Rail Ale Trail – these self-guided trails take you, on the branch lines, to pubs serving locally brewed ale and excellent food. Simply buy a return ticket and hop on and off as you go.

11
Blisland
A path less travelled

275m

259m

H

7km

2.5hrs

-3km

The focal point of this moorland walk is the recently cleaned and restored Jubilee Rock, a huge granite boulder that was carved in 1810 with patriotic insignia to celebrate the 50th anniversary of the coronation of King George III. It's a fascinating sight, but don't forget to turn around and enjoy the incredible views outward from this 215m vantage point. Keep your eyes peeled for the area's abundant wildlife, including foxes, deer and moorland ponies. The paths are not always clear on the moor, so it's a good idea to carry a map and compass with you and, in wet weather, when the ground can get boggy, wellies are a must. Do not attempt this challenging walk in fog.

11
Blisland
A path less travelled
Hantergantick
Delford Bridge
Hantergantick Granite Quarry
Disused Quarries
Quarry car park
Disused Quarries
Best's Penquite
South Penquite
Black Penquite
Lower Lank
Pump Building
South Kerrow
Pendrift Downs
Jubilee Rock
Pendrift
Tregenna
Tregenna Road
Lanxon
Tumrose
Lease
BLISLAND
Cassacawn
200m
500ft
8km
CLIMBS
275m
250m
225m
200m
175m
150m
1km
2km
3km
4km
5km
6km
7km

GETTING THERE

Blisland is a small village to the north of Bodmin and to the east of Wadebridge. It is signposted from the A30 northeast of Bodmin. Park on or near the village green and walk over to the Blisland Inn, one of our Pitstops, which is located next to the green. PL30 4JF.

WALK DIRECTIONS

1. Facing the Blisland Inn (see p.113), turn right and walk along the road, with the village green on your right. At the corner, follow the road around to the left and then carry on up the road, heading north (ignore the right turn). The lane gets smaller as it takes you gently uphill. When it bends sharply to the right after about 700m, turn off onto an even smaller (dead-end) lane straight ahead to Pendrift.

2. After a further 500m, you will cross over a cattle grid. Follow the lane around an initial bend and then go straight ahead through the gate and join the track. Here, views open up quickly. Follow down the right-hand border of two fields, go over the stile and down the hill, across the large field of bracken on the pathway. You will meet a footbridge.

NOT TO MISS

Rabbits, pheasants, foxes and deer

This area is thick with bracken, which provides welcome shelter to rabbits, pheasants, foxes and deer. Pheasants will often hide until you are almost upon them, before noisily flying away. Rabbits, on the other hand, will run at the mere sight of a human, beating a hasty retreat, tail in the air, followed swiftly by the rest of the colony.

SHORTCUT – This cuts off about half the route (but you still get to see Jubilee Rock), making a total walk length of just under 4km. In Instruction 2, when you reach Pendrift, keep going on the lane, past buildings and let it lead you to the right, whereupon it turns into a track. Follow straight ahead, passing some fields, until after about 150m you reach the moorland. You should see Jubilee Rock about 100m away, slightly over to the left. To orientate yourself back onto the route, face Jubilee Rock from the opposite side from where you arrived. Now skip to Instruction 7. (Be aware, the shortcut may be inaccessible due to farming activities. Be prepared to walk the full route!)

3. Cross over the small river on the footbridge and follow the path past the pump building and up the hill. Near the top of the hill, turn left then right to stay on the path. After 200m, turn left onto the driveway.

4. Almost immediately you arrive at a lane. Go straight over onto the indistinct path. Go straight ahead and, after 100m or so, veer right to follow alongside a fence on your right. After a further 150m or so, you will meet a track. Go over the stile on the right just here. Follow the path up to the top of the hill and turn right. Take a moment to admire the views. Now follow downhill (watch your footing on the steep and rocky parts) and you will quickly arrive at the parking area for a quarry.

5. Veer left in the parking area and walk ahead a few metres, then veer left again onto the track alongside the railing. Where the railing ends after only about 25m, you will see a tiny stone building on your left. Join the pathway just to the right of it and follow to the top of the hill, then let the yellow arrows guide you to a junction near a house. Turn right and walk a few metres down to the gate, after which you should walk through the woodland to a field. Once in the field, walk straight ahead to the driveway and turn right. When you meet the cattle grid after 250m or so, look for the stile on the right. Go over this and then cross the stream on the stepping stones (SX105747).

6. This is the moment to get out your map and compass, just in case, as Jubilee Rock (see below) can be a little difficult to find. From the stream, it is roughly SSW and our directions should hopefully get you there – but if you find it hard or are weary and want to get back, follow our alternative route below. (The rock is quite large, about 4m by 2m, and is visible on satellite imagery, if you have reception.)

TO FIND JUBILEE ROCK:

a) From the stream, walk ahead on the grassy path through the field ahead that is dotted with trees. You will notice some low banks after 100m or so that run perpendicular to the path – you will be walking through gaps in them.

b) When you pass the last bank, turn right onto the indistinct path, alongside it for the first 100m or so.

c) Keep following when the path veers slightly to the left, then at the junction turn right, past another low bank and into an area with gorse bushes.

d) The path forks after only 25m. Keep going straight ahead. The path will be quite small now. Follow it past small rocks and bushes until you see Jubilee Rock ahead of you. Take a moment to go up the carved steps at the back and admire the view.

ALTERNATIVE ROUTE – Instead of heading out onto the moor to find Jubilee Rock, turn left after crossing the stream and walk along the driveway until you reach a small lane. Turn right, follow around the sharp left-hand bend and then turn right at the next junction. Now walk down to the lane on the left and turn onto it. Skip to Instruction 8.

7 To continue from Jubilee Rock, face the rock from the direction you arrived. Walk past it and turn left onto the track (often muddy). Follow this and you will soon have an old wall on your right. Keep going straight when the track veers through the gate on the right and walk forward about 100m. You will see a large telegraph pole ahead of you. Walk towards it and at its base you will find a lane. Turn left, uphill, and walk about 150m to a right turn.

8 Take the right turn (if you are coming from the alternative route this is where you turn left). Follow along this narrow and pretty lane for about 300m then let it lead you right and downhill over a cattle grid. Follow all the way down to the T-junction and turn right to walk the final 750m into Blisland and the start point.

THE PITSTOPS

The Blisland Inn

This traditional real-ale pub (try the King Buddha), which has won several CAMRA (Campaign for Real Ale) awards, is known for its collections of beer mats, mugs and barometers, which festoon the bar. Although food isn't the focus here, the grub is seriously good, from Scotch eggs and pork pies at the bar to much fuller meals.

Blisland, Bodmin PL30 4JF. Open Mon–Fri 11.30–11.30, Sat 11.30–midnight, Sun midday–10.30. 01208 850739. www.bodminmoor.co.uk/blislandinn

Tredethy House

This lovingly restored country house, which dates back to Tudor times, is situated in an Area of Outstanding Natural Beauty. Its pop-up-style restaurant is a draw for hungry walkers. You can also stay the night here.

Tredethy, Bodmin PL30 4QS. Open Easter–Sep/Oct evenings; call ahead to book for large groups at lunchtime. 01208 841707. www.tredethyhouse.com

NOT TO MISS

Jubilee Rock

This massive granite rock, now a Grade II-listed monument, was first carved in 1810 by 24-year-old Lieutenant John Rogers, to celebrate the golden jubilee of King George III. Its patriotic emblems, carved into both of the sides as well as the top, include various coats of arms, the figure of Britannia, the Cornish emblem, a plough, a ship and a beehive. More carvings were added in 1887 to mark Queen Victoria's golden jubilee, and, in 2012, the monument was restored for the diamond jubilee of Queen Elizabeth II. Don't miss the two steps that allow you to climb to the top. (SX103743)

THE EXTRA STEP

Jamaica Inn, in fiction and in fact

Daphne du Maurier, who lived in Cornwall for more than three decades, set many of her novels in the county (see also p.90). From the intimate, tree-wrapped river estuaries of the south coast to the ruggedly beautiful upland moors, the writer was bewitched by the drama and romance of the Cornish landscape. And nowhere is this sense of place more explicit or more instantly recognisable than in her famous novel *Jamaica Inn* (1936), which is set on brooding Bodmin Moor.

The story follows a young woman, Mary, who leaves her home on the Helford River after the death of her mother to go and live with her aunt and uncle in their eerie and isolated public house on the edge of the moor. Mary soon realises that Jamaica Inn is a stop-off point for smugglers moving around their ill-gotten gains, and that her bullying uncle is part of a wrecking gang that lures ships onto the rocks with beacon lights on stormy nights in order to plunder the cargo. As the story unfolds, Mary gets drawn into the dark deeds of her uncle's lawless gang, against her will.

In this world-famous story, Du Maurier portrays Bodmin as a relentlessly bleak, even treacherous place. But she also seeks to reassure the reader about the 'real' Jamaica Inn in a note that accompanies the text: 'Jamaica Inn stands today, hospitable and kindly, a temperance house on the twenty-mile road between Bodmin and Launceston'. This stretch of road is known these days as the A30, and although Jamaica Inn is no longer a temperance house, it's a popular hotel, café and pub combined, as well as a fitting home for the Museum of Smuggling and a collection of Du Maurier memorabilia. The building is also said to be one of the most haunted places in Britain.

Bodmin's inhospitable side is as much a feature of the modern-day moor as it was when Du Maurier was writing. In November 2005, a freak snowstorm swept across the A30, leaving many motorists and lorry drivers stranded in their vehicles all night. The lucky ones were those who were able to seek shelter at Jamaica Inn, just as Du Maurier had done years before, when she and a companion got lost in the fog when out riding. Their sure-footed horses brought the pair safely back through the dark and dismal night to the old coaching house for a supper of eggs, bacon and tea.

12 Fox Tor and East Moor

Navigation by ancient monuments

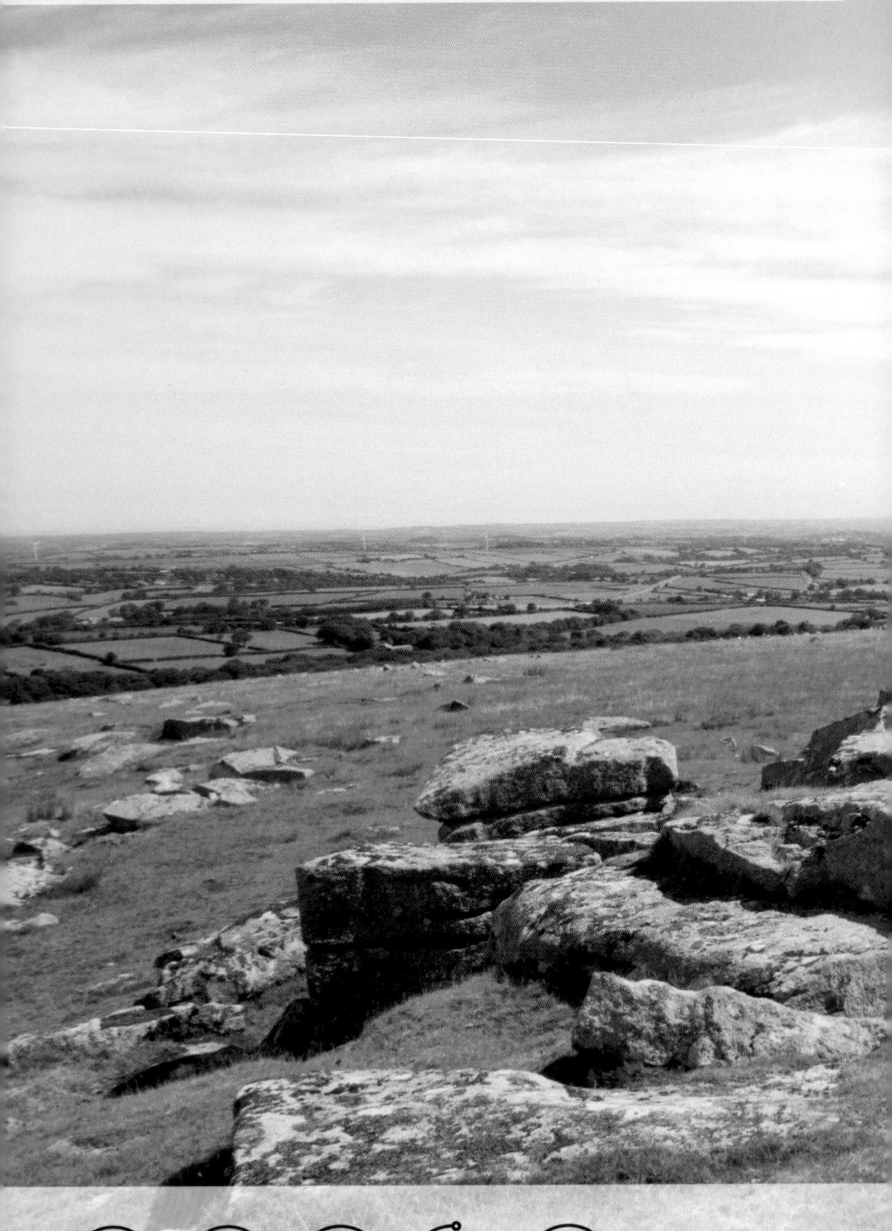

374m | 229m | M | 7km | 2.5hrs

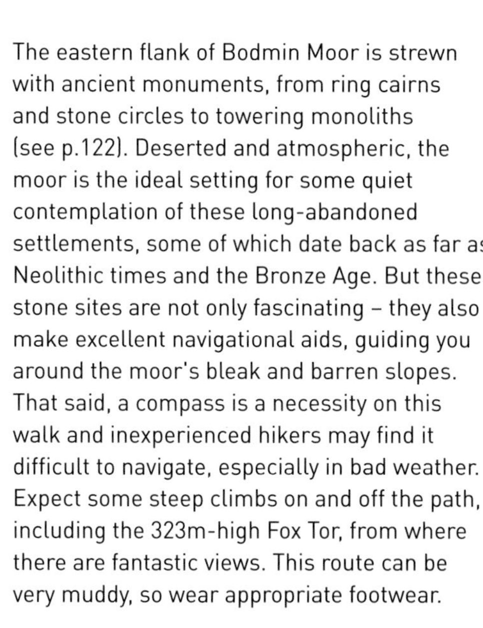

The eastern flank of Bodmin Moor is strewn with ancient monuments, from ring cairns and stone circles to towering monoliths (see p.122). Deserted and atmospheric, the moor is the ideal setting for some quiet contemplation of these long-abandoned settlements, some of which date back as far as Neolithic times and the Bronze Age. But these stone sites are not only fascinating – they also make excellent navigational aids, guiding you around the moor's bleak and barren slopes. That said, a compass is a necessity on this walk and inexperienced hikers may find it difficult to navigate, especially in bad weather. Expect some steep climbs on and off the path, including the 323m-high Fox Tor, from where there are fantastic views. This route can be very muddy, so wear appropriate footwear.

12 Fox Tor and East Moor

Navigation by ancient monuments

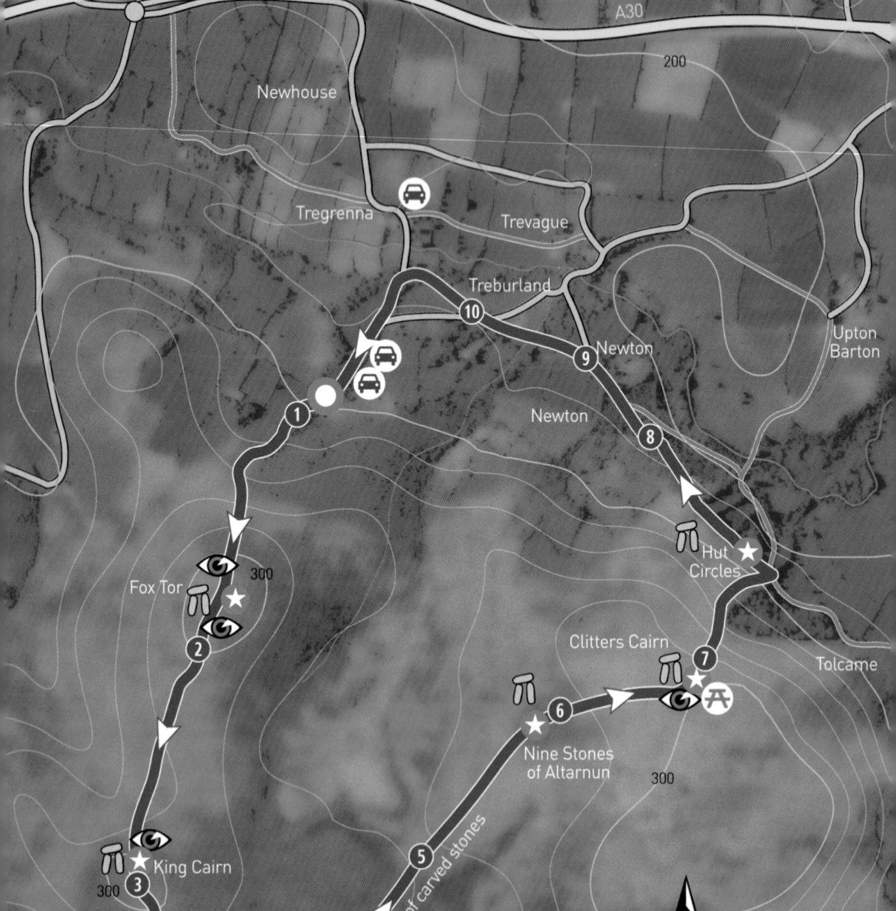

Five Lanes
Trewint
A30
200
Newhouse
Tregrenna
Trevague
Treburland
10
9
Newton
Upton Barton
1
Newton
8
Hut Circles
300
Fox Tor
2
Clitters Cairn
7
Tolcarne
6
Nine Stones of Altarnun
300
King Cairn
3
300
5
Series of carved stones
N
300m
1,000ft
Greymare Rock
4

CLIMBS

375m
350m
325m
300m
275m
250m
1km
2km
3km
4km
5km
6km
7km

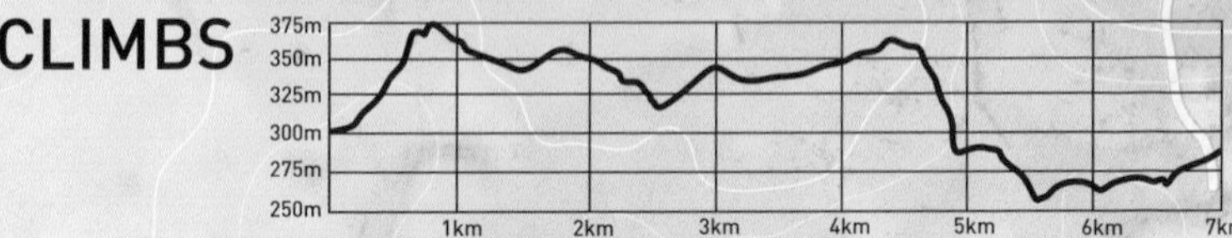

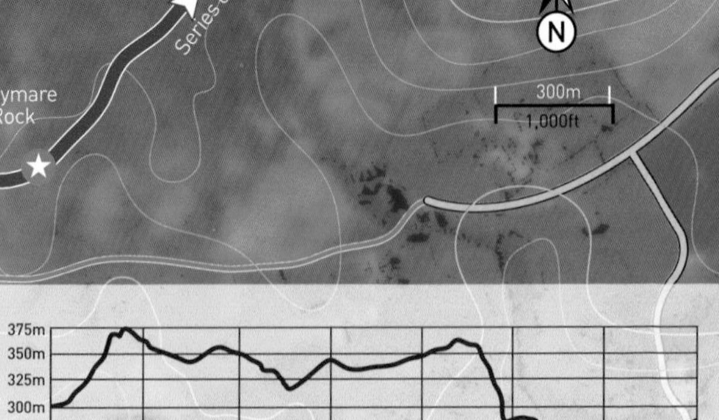

GETTING THERE

Travelling southwest on the A30 out of Launceston, or northeast on the A30 out of Bodmin, take the exit for Fivelanes or Altarnun on a section of dual carriageway. Go to the roundabout to the south of the A30 and take the first exit, towards Trevague. At a sharp bend to the left, keep going straight ahead onto a dead-end road. Follow this narrow lane around bends and down into the valley and over the large stream. Once you are driving uphill again, start looking for a suitable place to park on the verge. Do not worry if you park quite far up – the route includes this lane at the beginning. At the top of the hill, the lane bends to the right and becomes a private driveway. If you cannot find a place to park without blocking field entrances, passing places or the lane, go back up the other side of the valley and park on one of the flat grassy areas to the side of the road. PL15 7SB.

WALK DIRECTIONS

1. Walk up the lane to the top of the hill, where it turns into a private driveway as described above. Turn off onto the track straight ahead and you will soon arrive at a gate. Go through and follow the track as it bends to the left uphill. Turn off the track to the left just after the stream, and head for the higher ground of Fox Tor (SX226785) – you might pick up a pathway. As you near the top, head for the large rocks and you will see the shaped trig point marking the top.

2. After soaking up the superb views from the trig point, continue in the same direction, a tiny bit west of south, towards King Cairn (SX223776). There is a stone row that leads to King Cairn – it's hard to distinguish from all the other rocks, but comprises pyramid-shaped rocks about 50 to 100m apart. The hill gently ascends to King Cairn, which is a grassy circle of bumps – slightly indistinct but obvious once you have found it.

NOT TO MISS

Hut circles

Admittedly, some imagination is required to discern the remains of these prehistoric settlements, but ancient roundhouse formations can be seen clearly throughout this route. They are said to date from around the 2nd century BC.

Stone rows and boundary stones

Though the purpose of Neolithic stone rows is unclear, it's been suggested that they might mark religious processional routes. Boundary stones, as the name suggest, mark the borders of land.

Stone circles

These monuments are almost certainly sites of religious ritual, with the placement of the stones often having significant celestial alignment.

Cairns and ring cairns

These piles of stones, which date mainly from the Bronze Age, are thought to have had a variety of uses in prehistoric ceremonies – a subject that remains, however, a source of much speculation today. What is known is that many of the stones have been appropriated for other purposes, such as buildings, dry-stone walls and laying roads.

THE PITSTOP

Rising Sun Inn

This delightful 16th-century inn, set right on the edge of the moor, is a traditional country pub serving local ales – many of which are brewed in Altarnun itself – and good square meals. Fresh bread is made here every day, sometimes twice a day. The pub's small campsite is ideal if you want to bed down for the night.

Altarnun, PL15 7SN. Open Mon–Fri noon–2.30 & 5.30–11, Sat/Sun noon–11/10. 01566 86636
www.therisingsuninn.co.uk

3 After King Cairn, head SSE to another nearby cairn (this one with visible rocks) and keep going on the same bearing. The large hump shape of Greymare Rock (SX225772) will be visible further down the hill.

4 At Greymare Rock, orientate yourself so that you have the rock at your back and King Cairn uphill to your left. About 20m away there are two large rocks (usually in a pool of standing water). Walk in a direction with these rocks a few meters to the right (walk east) and keep going on the same bearing to walk down a gentle hill into a smooth, wide, grassy valley. Here, look for some small standing stones. There should be one over to the right next to a larger rock and two others heading off in a line to the left. Turn left to follow the bearing that the two on the left give you. You will be walking northeast. (If you can't see the stones, don't worry, simply walk NE from the grassy valley.)

5 After a while you will notice Fox Tor diagonally to the left. Once it is almost level to your left, you should be able to see the famous stone circle the Nine Stones of Altarnun (SX235781) ahead of you.

6 Continuing in the same direction from the stone circle, you will see two small standing stones, quite prominent, ahead of you at 250m and 300m away. Walk to the second one and then turn diagonally to your right. Walk over to Clitters Cairn (SX241782), which is a prominent rocky mound on the near horizon with a lone, windswept tree bravely growing from its top. This is an ideal picnic spot with astonishing views.

7 From Clitters Cairn walk north, roughly left from where you arrived, down a steep hill to a wooded area surrounded by an old wall. As you near the wood, veer left to the corner and follow downhill with the wall on your right. Keep following the border wall when it turns to the left and walk on roughly level ground to the next corner. Here, turn with the border to the right briefly but then almost immediately turn left to follow a hidden track diagonally downhill (over-run by gorse bushes).

8 After 250m or so, you will arrive at a stream. Turn left and walk about 50m to turn right over a stile into a wood. Turn left and walk along two sides of the wood to the gate and stile. Go over onto the lane.

9 Turn right onto the lane and after about 100m, turn off onto a path to the left and walk past the telegraph pole and down the left-hand side of a tree plantation. After about 150m, you will arrive at an open area. Walk straight ahead to the bottom and into another small wood. You should find a stile and stepping stones over the stream. Walk towards the farmhouse in the field and over another stile onto the driveway. Walk past the farmhouse (on your left).

10 About 100m after the farmhouse, go over the stone steps (over the wall) on your right. Walk diagonally left across the field to the far bottom corner near the trees. Go over the stile and down the steps onto the lane. You are now on the lower part of the lane you started on – near the large stream. Simply walk to where you parked to finish off the route.

THE EXTRA STEP

Bodmin Moor and the mystery of prehistory

Bodmin Moor may these days be a wild and largely uninhabited expanse of open moorland, but there's a wealth of evidence to suggest it was once a hub of civilisation, as this walk, with its ritual sites and settlements, so vividly attests. The great mystery is why such an inhospitable granite landscape attracted our ancient ancestors in the first place. The answer is probably because, 10,000 years ago, when it was covered with dense forest and roamed by hunter-gatherers, it was not nearly such a bleak place. Fast-forward a few thousand years, to the Neolithic period, and people flocked here to cut down trees to make way for farmland. It was around this time, and slightly later, during the Bronze Age, that many of the landmarks we see today were built.

The main megalithic monuments on Bodmin Moor – in addition to those mentioned in this walk – include the 4,000-year-old Stripple Stones, Britain's largest stone circle, and the 3,500-year-old Hurlers, a line of three stones situated between the Lynher and Fowey rivers. Legend has it that these were once men who had been turned to stone as punishment for playing the Celtic game of hurling on a Sunday. Both of these sets of standing stones can be reached on foot from a car park a few miles southwest of the village of Minions. Other vestiges of these age-old communities include the occasional fragment of prehistoric field system and Trevethy Quoit, also near Minions, one of twenty Neolithic portal tombs that survive in the world today.

But by far the most mysterious of all of the ancient remains on Bodmin Moor is King Arthur's Hall, which is situated on King Arthur's Downs, just north of the A30. Thought to date from the Neolithic period or early Bronze Age, the site consists of 56 vertical stones arranged around the inside edge of a rectangular enclosure – these upright stones bear an uncanny resemblance to the tall backs of chairs, which probably explains the name. Theories abound as to the exact function of this 4,500-year-old formation, which was linked to the nearby village of St Breward by an ancient footpath. Some insist it was a ceremonial site, while others say it was merely a cattle pound. The truth is that we'll probably never know.

13 Trebarwith and Tregardock

Where the west wind blows

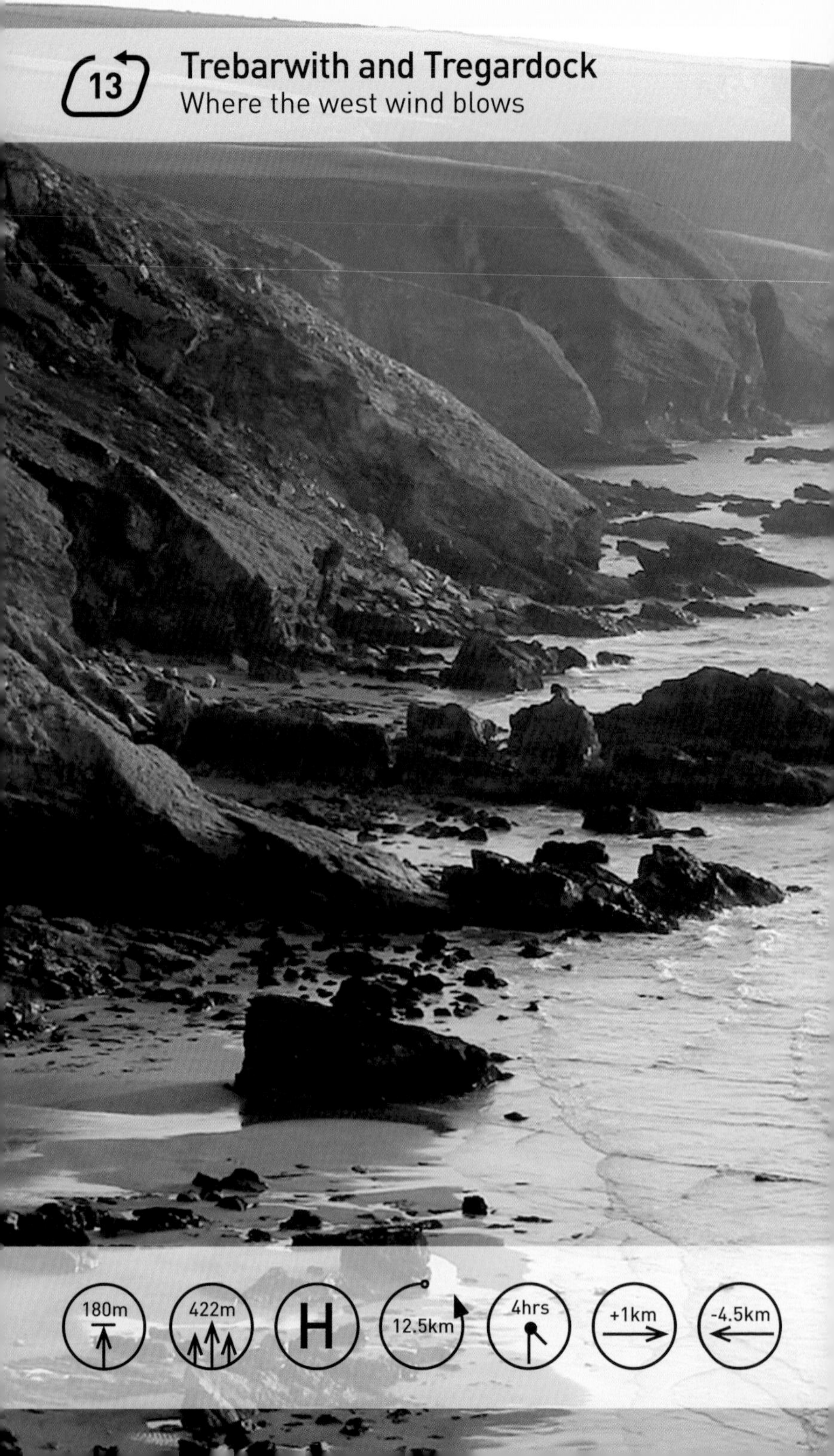

It only takes a few moments on wild, west-facing Tregardock beach to realise that this stretch of coast takes a regular pounding from raging Atlantic storms. The headland looks as though it's on the verge of collapse – caves and overhangs have been smashed out of the base of the cliffs and juggernaut-sized boulders lie tossed around the stream-crossed golden sands as though they're mere pebbles. Even the mussels and barnacles that cling to the rocks here seem to have a grim determination to their grip. As well as this beauty spot, our suggested walk takes in several steep ascents before leading you back along winding paths through some of Cornwall's most beautiful countryside.

13
Trebarwith and Tregardock
Where the west wind blows
Tregatta
Hole Beach
Treknow
B3263
Trelake
Trebarwith Strand
Trebarwith Strand
Gull Rock
Dennis Point
100
Trebarwith
N
300m
2,000ft
Besloe
Trecarne Farm
Trebarwith R
Downhouse
Trecarne
100
Flat Hole
Stone Quarry
Tregonnick Tail
Treligga
200
Tregardock Beach
Tregonnick
Tregardock
200
B3314
Tregragon
Jacket's Point
100
Westdowns
B3267
Crookmoyle Rock
Dannonchapel
1
2
3
4
5
6
7
8
9
CLIMBS
175m
150m
125m
100m
75m
50m
25m
1km
2km
3km
4km
5km
6km
7km
8km
9km
10km
11km
12km
13km
Lower Tynes
Dinnabroad
200

GETTING THERE

Trebarwith Strand is well signposted from the B3263, just south of Tintagel. In winter, you can park alongside the road on the yellow lines for free, but please check signs. There are also two car parks on the right as you arrive. We recommend the first, as the second can get congested due to the narrow lane. PL34 0HB.

WALK DIRECTIONS

❶ Starting in the main car park, turn right on the lane and walk about 250m downhill, then fork left up towards the pub (see p.133). Just before the pub, turn left into the parking area and at the far end go over the stile and turn right onto the coast path to walk uphill.

❷ Walk to the top of the headland and continue over. On the way out of the first deep valley along this section, look for the short pathway to a lovely viewpoint and picnic spot within the ruins of an old slate building.

❸ After about 3km on the coast path, you will cross over a slate footbridge and reach a path crossways. Straight ahead is the continuation of the route, right is an optional extra to Tregardock Beach and picnic spots on the headland overlooking it, and left is a shortcut.

OPTIONAL EXTRA – It's quite a long way down to Tregardock Beach but well worth the effort if you're feeling like the extra challenge. Follow the path all the way there and back, taking note of the flat picnic areas.

SHORTCUT – Turning left at the junction after the slate footbridge will shorten the route to about 8km in total. Simply follow the well-used pathway for about 250m until you reach a junction in the corner of a field. Turn left to follow the right-hand field border and the yellow arrows. Jump to Instruction 6.

❹ Continuing the full route, keep going on the coast path towards Dannon Chapel. After about 1.5km and just after a small footbridge, turn left over the stile and onto the pathway heading inland to Tregragon. Follow the field edges all the way to the farm and then join the farm driveway.

❺ After about 500m on the farm driveway and about 100m before a T-junction, go over the double stile on the left and onto a footpath directly across the field – head for the gap in the field border on the far side. In the next field, walk along the right-hand edge, go through the gate and turn left on the lane to walk downhill. After about 300m, between two farm buildings, turn right onto the footpath signposted towards the coast path.

6 After 250m, you reach a field. Go straight ahead, following yellow arrows along the right-hand edge of several fields. This is where the shortcut comes out. After the fields, you reach a track that leads straight ahead to a lane in Treligga. Turn left, follow around the bend to the right and turn left again. After about 100m, turn left a third time and walk along the dead-end road.

7 The lane turns into a track and you soon arrive at a farm. After the first couple of buildings, you will see a signposted pathway on your right. Follow this along two left-hand field edges. Walk directly across the third field towards the buildings and go through the gate on the left – there should be a yellow mark on the gate post. Now go through the kissing gate on the coastal side of the large building.

THE PITSTOPS

The Port William

Nestled into the cliffs overlooking Trebarwith Strand, the Port William is known for its excellent food and real ales, and fabulous coastal views. Sit in the big-windowed bar or conservatory, or on the terrace if it's sunny, to make the most of one of North Cornwall's most spectacular settings. Trebarwith Strand, Trebarwith PL34 0HB. Open Mon–Sat 8.30–11, Sun 8.30–10.30. 01840 770230. www.theportwilliam.co.uk

The Strand Café

This café, which lies just metres from stunning Trebarwith Strand, serves up a delicious selection of sandwiches, burgers, salads and homemade cakes to a distinctly windblown clientele. The walls of this tiny building act as an exhibition space for local artists, many of whom are regulars. The vibe is so relaxed and informal, you can hang out here for hours or grab a drink to go. Trebarwith Strand PL34 0HB. Open summer 10–5.30 (closed Mon in term time), winter occasional weekends. 01840 779482. www.thestrandcafe.co.uk

8 Now follow more yellow arrows through fields, over a stream and up a steep hill to a lane. Turn left and this will take you a couple of hundred metres into Trebarwith village.

9 Stay on the lane through the village and, just opposite Trebarwith Farm, turn left onto the signposted pathway. You will walk along a farm track for about 300m until a sharp, left-hand bend. Just here, fork right onto a pathway. This path will take you all the way down to Trebarwith Strand, where you arrive in the pub car park where you joined the coast path near the beginning of the walk. At the end of the pub car park, turn right and walk back to where you parked and started the walk. Don't forget about our two Pitstops (see below), offering refuge and refreshments for weary walkers.

THE EXTRA STEP

The grey gold of Delabole

Delabole, which is named after its enormous quarry, is synonymous with slate. The rock has been mined in the village since the 15th century, making its slate quarry – originally five separate pits and now one big one – the oldest working one of its kind in the country.

In Elizabethan times, when slate became a popular roofing material, the quarry took on considerable importance, supplying the rock across the country and to such faraway places as Brittany and the Netherlands. As towns and cities grew throughout the Industrial Revolution, demand and output for this grey gold increased. By the middle of the 19th century, 1,000 men were employed here, raising around 120 tonnes of slate every day. Before the advent of the railways, the rock was hauled to nearby Port Gaverne, where women helped stow it safely aboard boats that were destined for ports all over the world.

The consequence of so much activity over so long a time is a very large hole in the ground; today, it measures 125m deep and nearly a kilometre across. These days, 120 tonnes of slate is still raised every day, but – thanks to modern equipment and techniques – this is done by five quarrymen, rather than 1,000. After a recent management buyout, the future of the mine seems assured, with reserves set to last 300 years. And although slate is now far too expensive for most roofing, it's in great demand as a decorative material, either in its smoky-grey natural form or polished to a gleaming black finish.

But there's more to Delabole than slate. This large village, which was actually three hamlets until the railway arrived in 1893, is home to Britain's first commercial wind farm, the Cornwall Air Ambulance and one of the biggest carnivals in the county. It also lies within an Area of Outstanding Natural Beauty – in other words, it's an industrial powerhouse on a breathtakingly beautiful stretch of coastline.

14 Boscastle

Witches, woodlands and scenic waterways

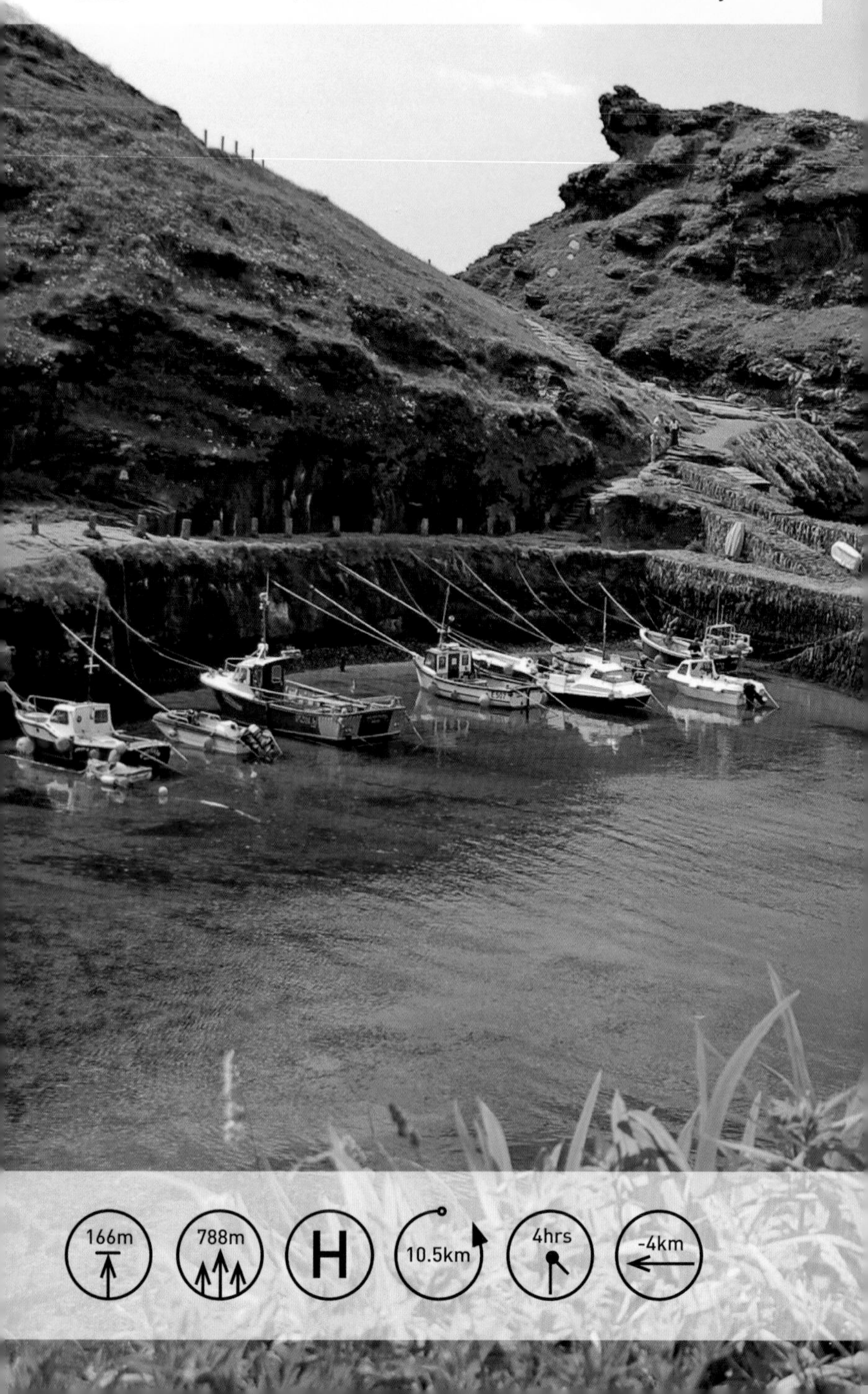

166m | 788m | H | 10.5km | 4hrs | -4km

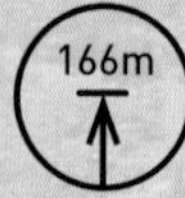

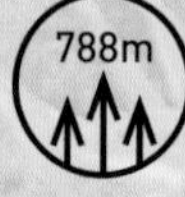

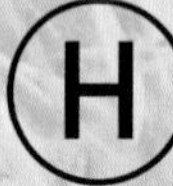

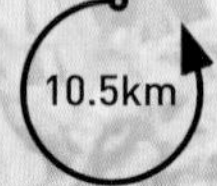

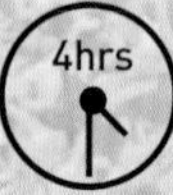

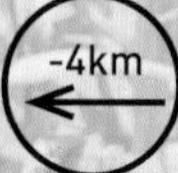

The picturesque beauty of the wooded valleys surrounding the coastal village and fishing port of Boscastle is truly breathtaking, making this one of the most memorable walks in the book. The village itself, which was devastated by a flash flood in 2004, has now recovered and has lots to offer visitors, including a pretty, natural harbour with two 16th-century harbour walls, a fascinating Museum of Witchcraft, which comprises artefacts dating from prehistory to the present day, and two celebrated churches. The walk itself has some very steep sections – it contains one of the most challenging parts of the South West Coast Path – and is quite long, taking in both coast and inland paths and revealing stunning views. There are two shortcuts if you want to shorten the route and avoid some of the hills.

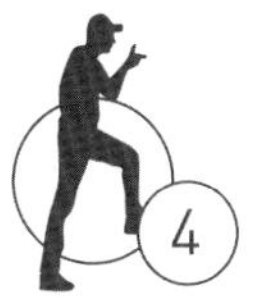

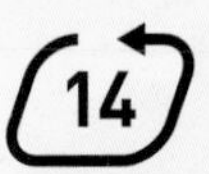

14 Boscastle

Witches, woodlands and scenic waterways

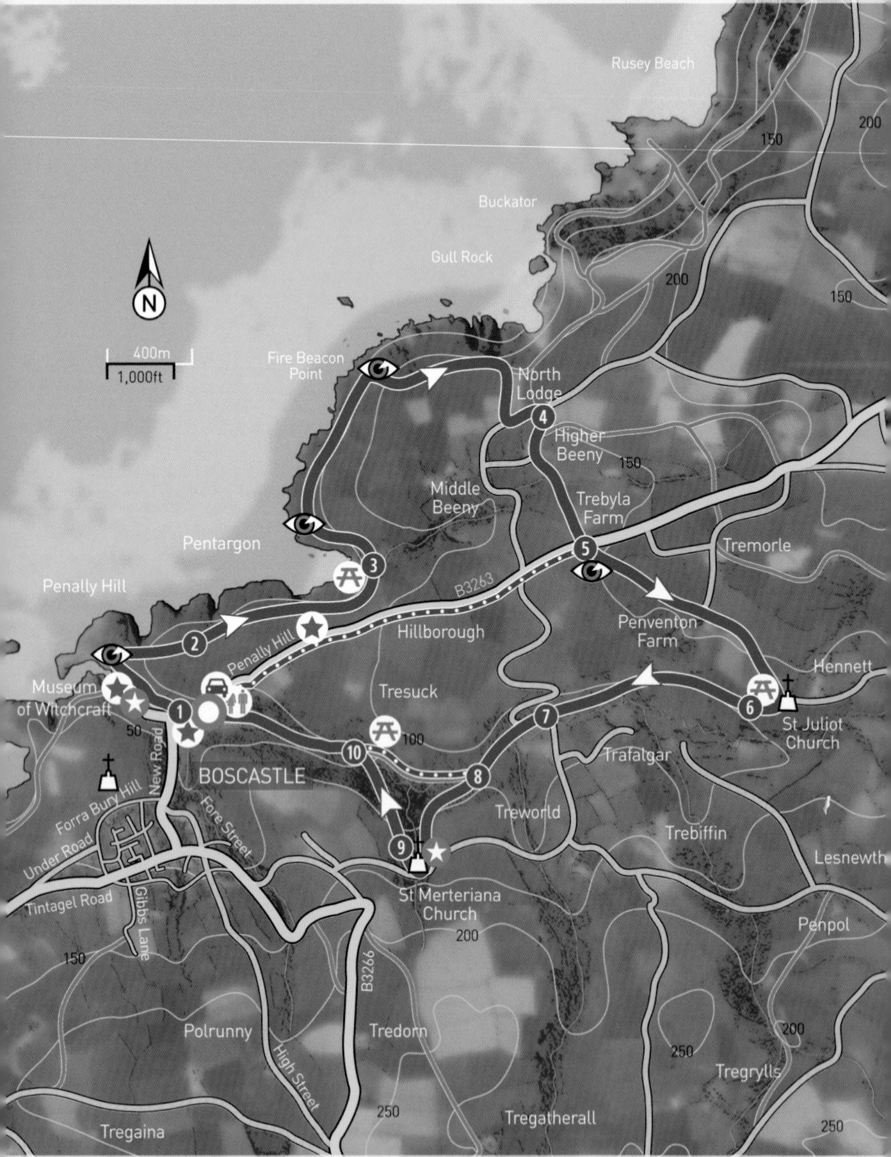
The Strangles
Voter Run
Rusey Beach
Buckator
Gull Rock
N
400m
1,000ft
Fire Beacon Point
North Lodge
Higher Beeny
Middle Beeny
Trebyla Farm
Pentargon
Tremorle
Penally Hill
B3263
Penventon Farm
Hillborough
Penally Hill
Hennett
Museum of Witchcraft
Tresuck
St Juliot Church
Trafalgar
New Road
BOSCASTLE
Forra Bury Hill
Fore Street
Treworld
Trebiffin
Under Road
St Merteriana Church
Lesnewth
Tintagel Road
Gibbs Lane
Penpol
B3266
Polrunny
Tredorn
High Street
Tregrylls
Tregatherall
Tregaina
Cardew

CLIMBS

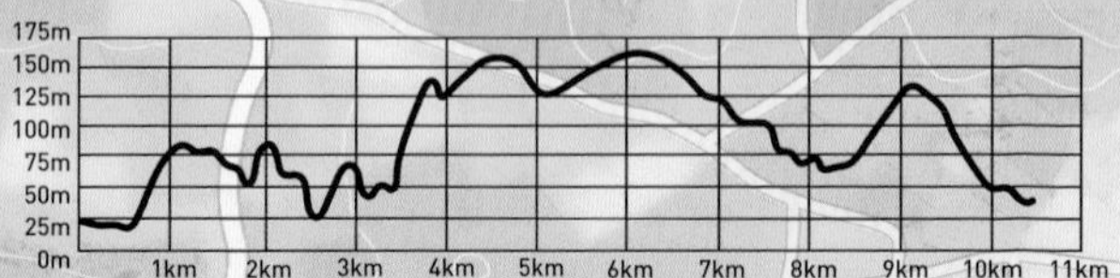
175m
150m
125m
100m
75m
50m
25m
0m
1km
2km
3km
4km
5km
6km
7km
8km
9km
10km
11km

GETTING THERE

Boscastle is easy to find on the north Cornish coast near Tintagel. When you arrive in the village, follow signs to the harbour. The main car park is on Penally Hill (B3263), opposite the Cobweb Inn and next to the post office. In winter you can park on certain yellow lines instead of in the car park – check the signs though, as this is subject to change. PL35 0HE.

WALK DIRECTIONS

1. Leaving from the car park entrance, turn left and walk towards the harbour, keeping the river on your left. At the Harbour Light Tea Garden (see p.140), fork right uphill on the lane. Walk up to and past the terrace of cottages, then join the coast path. Be sure to enjoy the magnificent views of this natural inlet and unspoilt harbour, with its Elizabethan quay surrounded by steep cliffs and blowholes.

SHORTCUT #1 – The first section of coast path that runs along Beeny Cliff has an imposing reputation. If you would like to avoid this but still enjoy the inland hills, streams and views, walk up Penally Hill (B3263) for about 2.5km and pick up the route from Instruction 5 at Trebyla Farm.

2. Follow the coast path for just over 1km. Soon after the waterfall comes into view, you have the option of venturing across a field to Boscastle Farm Shop (see p.140), where you can buy supplies for a picnic. Next, you will descend steps into a deep valley. Just before the footbridge, go down the small path on the left to see the waterfall up close. There is a small, grassy picnic area here, albeit for those with a head for heights.

3. Continuing on the coast path, in the next valley ignore the right turn. You will now be on Beeny Cliff. Walk along and after the long climb to the top, you will enter some fields. Follow the path that's roughly level with the left-hand border and on the far side of the third field, turn right, inland, before the kissing gate. (It's a marked path.) Walk to the lane and turn left, walking past North Lodge.

4. Just after passing North Lodge, turn right down the lane to Higher Beeny and after the main collection of farm buildings (and opposite the farmhouse), turn right onto a rutted track and walk 50m downhill to a gate and stile. Go over this, into the field, and walk diagonally across to the border at the bottom of the hill. Go through the gate, over the footbridge and then walk directly ahead up the hill in the next field. You will walk through a small campsite. You are now at Trebyla Farm. Turn right on the farm track and follow it to the road (B3263). This is where Shortcut #1 joins the main route.

THE PITSTOPS

Boscastle Farm Shop

Boscastle Farm Shop stocks a fantastic range of local and organic produce, including plenty to stock a packed lunch or picnic. Stop by at the on-site café, if you have time. The coastal views are superb. Hillsborough Farm, Boscastle PL35 0HH. Open 9–4 (café), 9–5 (shop). 01840 250827. www.boscastlefarmshop.co.uk

The Harbour Light Tea Garden

This popular café boasts a fantastic position right on the harbour, just across from the Museum of Witchcraft. Expect great light meals, attentive staff and the tastiest ice cream in the village. The Harbour, Boscastle PL35 0HD. Open daily 10–4. 01840 250953

The Riverside

The third option for this walk, as the name and address suggest, is located next to the harbour bridge in the centre of Boscastle. Surrounded by tea (and witch) shops, it's a welcome white-tablecloth alternative for hungry walkers. With pleasing prices and generous portions, the day or evening menu will satisfy most people's tastes or requirements.
The Bridge, Boscastle PL35 0HE. 01840 250216
www.hotelriverside.co.uk

5 Cross straight over the road, up the steps and into the field. You now walk southeast on a path through five fields separated by stiles and kissing gates. (First field, walk diagonally left. Second field, walk to the far left corner. Third field, go straight to the stile about 50m to the right of the gate. Fourth field, diagonally right to the kissing gate in the corner. Fifth field, along the left-hand edge and over the stile.) You will now be on a farm track. Turn left, walk 50m, go over another stile, turn left again, walk 20m to the lane and turn right. This will lead you to St Juliot, a 15th-century church that underwent major restoration work in the 19th century (see p.144). Roughly halfway, it's a good place to stop for a picnic – you should find a nice spot in or around the churchyard.

6 After exploring the churchyard, join the path on the opposite side from where you entered. Walk diagonally right to a stile and over into fields. Walk west along this path – the first two fields along the left edge, the third field across to the gate and the fourth along the right edge to enter the woods. Walk all the way through the woods and you will eventually arrive at a driveway.

7 Turn right, walk uphill 50m to a lane, then turn left to walk downhill. Fork right almost straight away and follow the track down to the gate. Walk past the pretty cottage and continue onto the path alongside the river. After a few hundred metres, you will reach a footbridge.

SHORTCUT #2 – With all these hills and valleys, you may be weary by this point. Although it's well worth the effort, if you don't feel you can tackle the hill up to St Merteriana church, then simply carry on along the river to return to the car park in Boscastle.

8 Cross the footbridge and follow the path up through the woods. Near the top, fork left and you will find St Merteriana easily enough.

9 At the church, find the path that runs along below the graveyard. It is a level path – do not descend the steps down to the stream. After 150m, turn right to follow downhill for over 300m into the valley to the river.

10 As you approach the river, veer left then, after 100m, you will see stepping stones on the right. Go over these; this is where Shortcut #2 rejoins the route. Look right to see the large grassy field, which is perfect for a picnic near the end of the walk. Or turn left to follow the river back to Boscastle and finish the walk. NOTE: Don't forget to visit the Heritage Centre, where there's a detailed account of the devastation caused by the 2004 flood and how the village survived. Afterwards, head into the regenerated high street to visit the artisanal shops, which feature works by local artists and crafts people. And don't miss the Museum of Witchcraft (see opposite), down on the harbour, which houses the world's largest collection of Wicca artefacts.

NOT TO MISS

St Merteriana church (Minster Church)

This Norman minster, which was erected in 1150 and restored in both the 16th and 19th centuries, has many of its original details still intact. During the spring, the graveyard, where the ground is no doubt very fertile, is covered in wild garlic. Whether you choose to cook with it is entirely up to you, but it's certainly a pretty sight.

NOT TO MISS

Museum of Witchcraft

The Wicca artefacts on display in this superb museum date from prehistory to contemporary times. Remarkably, they survived the 2004 floods relatively unscathed, despite the museum building being badly damaged. At the time, the museum owner was a volunteer coastguard and had to choose to save the villagers or the museum's contents; of course, he chose the former. As luck would have it, though, the rushing water pushed nearly all the museum artefacts into one corner, where they remained undamaged.
The Harbour, Boscastle PL35 0HD. Open summer Mon–Sat/Sun 10.30/11.30–6, winter times vary. www.museumofwitchcraft.com

THE EXTRA STEP

Thomas Hardy, loves old and new

The latter part of our route passes through the Valency Valley, which is at its most picturesque between the half-forgotten church of St Juliot and the harbourside village of Boscastle. Though the valley is splendid at any time of year, it's particularly lovely in spring, when the brook babbles past banks of primroses, carpets of bluebells and grass flecked with wood anemones. In the summer, wildflower meadows burst into life here, drawing butterflies in their fluttering droves. In 1870, a young architect and writer named Thomas Hardy came to St Juliot to plan the restoration of the parish church. Here, he fell in love with the wilderness of the Valency Valley and with Emma Gifford, the rector's sister-in-law. The two were married in 1874 and Hardy's early novel *A Pair of Blue Eyes* is based on their romance.

Sadly, it was not the happiest of marriages. The couple were driven to living on separate floors in the same house in the later years of their union, until Emma's death in 1912. Their story has a curious afterlife, however. After Emma's death, Hardy was overcome with remorse at the course their relationship had taken and produced some of the finest love poems in the English language in her memory. His 1912 poem 'The Voice' encapsulates this sense of intense longing and regret, opening with the line: 'Woman much missed, how you call to me, call to me'. Hardy returned to the parish of St Juliot the following spring to reflect on those distant happy days of youthful courtship. There, he designed a memorial tablet to his late wife, which was made by a local stonemason and can still be seen on the church's north wall. Hardy married his secretary, Florence, in 1914, but never shook off his complex sense of grief at Emma's passing.

In the church, there's a fine engraved window by Simon Whistler, son of the celebrated glass engraver Laurence Whistler. The window, which was commissioned by the Thomas Hardy Society to celebrate the millennium and dedicated in 2003, depicts three of Hardy's poems. One of these, 'Under the Waterfall', tells of the moment when, during a picnic in the Valency Valley, Hardy and Emma lost a drinking glass in the stream.

In many ways, the parish of St Juliot shaped Hardy's life, and the church that he saved from rack and ruin all those years ago is today a fitting memorial to one of Britain's best-loved novelists and poets.

Poundstock and Millook Haven

Calm in the countryside

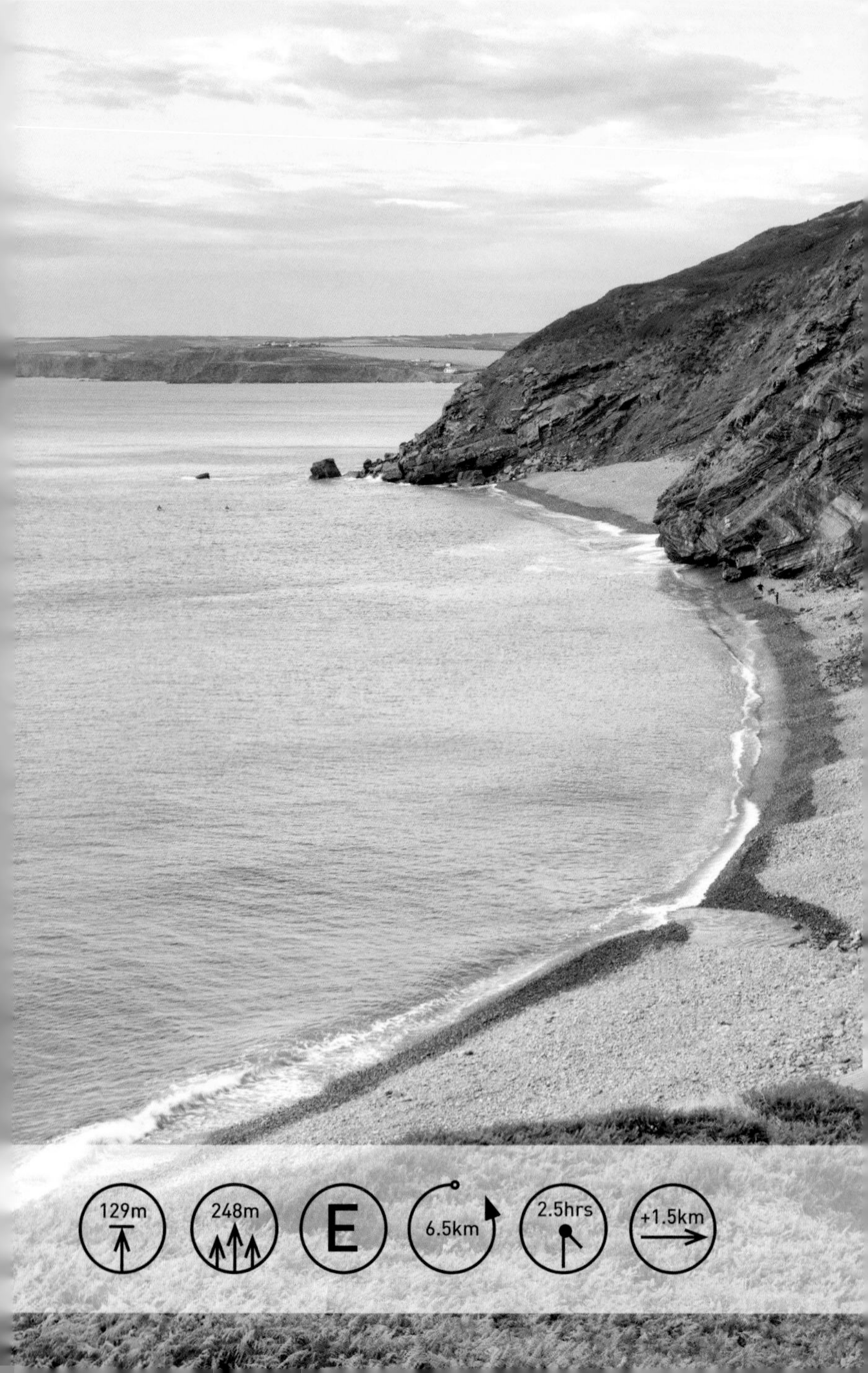

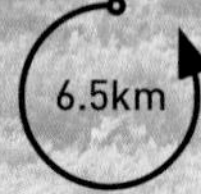

This is a simple walk down country lanes, along footpaths with overgrown hedgerows and through magnificent open countryside. There are no steep climbs, although there is an optional stretch that leads down to the quiet, pebbly beach at Millook Haven, famous for its rock formations. History buffs will love the medieval church and adjacent, Grade I-listed church house, which, remarkably, has been in continuous use since it was built in Tudor times. The route can get muddy in parts, so make sure you wear sensible footwear.

15 Poundstock and Millook Haven

Calm in the countryside

CLIMBS

GETTING THERE

Poundstock is a village located near the coast, about halfway between Boscastle and Bude. Turn off the A39 onto Vicarage Lane, following the signs to the church. The lane becomes very narrow, but you'll soon see the cemetery car park on your left. EX23 0AU.

WALK DIRECTIONS

1. Walk out of the car park and turn left down the lane. After 100m, go through the second kissing gate into the churchyard. Walk past the church, and out onto the lane next to a small row of old terraced cottages. Turn left and follow the stream on your left briefly, before heading uphill on the lane for about 100m. Just next to a white thatched cottage, turn right onto a footpath. It looks like the cottage driveway, but walk past the side of the cottage and you'll see the path to the left. (If you walk past the turning and look back, you'll see the footpath sign.)

NOT TO MISS

St Winwaloe church and Poundstock Gildhouse

The medieval church of St Winwaloe, with its battlemented bell tower, has undergone extensive restoration over the centuries, as has the adjacent Poundstock Gildhouse. This Grade I-listed church house, which has been in continual use for 500 years, is one of the most finely restored examples of its kind in the county. The building was designed to be an extension of the church, containing a feasting hall, schoolhouse and meeting rooms at various times over the centuries.

2. Follow the path for 150m to a lane. Go straight ahead (right) and keep going for just under a kilometre, first downhill and then uphill. Just before an old cattle grid, you'll see a track that leads off to the left. Take this and after 300m, it turns into a path. Keep following it for a further 400m through hedgerows until you reach a farm lane.

3. You now enter a hamlet and farm called Tregole. Go right onto the track, which is more of a tiny lane, almost doubling back on yourself. Follow this until you reach Longland farm.

4. At the farm, join the footpath on the left just before the barn. Cross over to the gate at the midpoint of the opposite boundary, and then follow the path (at times indistinct) along the right-hand edge of the next field to the stile. Follow the small path down into the woods to a footbridge.

5. Go over the footbridge and follow the path for about 300m to a lane, almost a track. Turn right and walk uphill. After about 250m, turn left onto the footpath to walk downhill into the valley. At the time of writing, there was an overgrown bench about 50m before the turning. This pathway leads you to a house where there is a ford over a stream. Go over the stream and continue on the track. After 750m, you will arrive at the first few houses in Millook.

OPTIONAL EXTRA – To visit the beach at Millook Haven (see below), keep going on the track, go through the gate then downhill for a short distance on the lane to the sea. It's a beautiful spot for a rest or a picnic and is almost exactly halfway along the route.

NOT TO MISS

Millook Haven

The cliffs that fringe this quiet pebbled beach were voted by the Geological Society of London to be one of the top 10 geological sites in Britain. If you look closely, you'll be able to see the folding layers of rock that make them so remarkable.

6 After the first few houses in Millook, go over the footbridge on the right and follow the footpath up the short hill, along the left-hand field edge and into the woods. Now walk for 500m in some very pretty woodland. Cross over another footbridge when you reach it and walk uphill into the field. Walk straight across the field to the top of the hill, then head for the gate. Be sure to look behind you for some exceptional views.

7 Go through the kissing gate on the far side of the field and walk ahead on the track (left). After about 300m, the track turns into a lane and you go over a bridge. Keep going for roughly 500m and you arrive at a junction. Go straight ahead (left) and walk past the church to find the car park where you started the walk.

THE PITSTOPS

Bangors Organics

The well-stocked shop at Bangors is a great place to buy picnic ingredients, while the restaurant is perfect for a good meal after a long day on foot. Expect the freshest home-grown produce. Bangors House, Poundstock, Bude EX23 0DP. Open Thu–Sat 11–4 (shop); 7–late, booking only (restaurant). 01288 361297 www.bangorsorganic.co.uk

Widemouth Manor Hotel

Fresh produce from local farmers and fishermen fills the menu at the restaurant in this hotel, where you can sit out on the beautiful terrace on sunny days. If you feel like splashing out, stay the night, wake up to the sound of the sea and book up a spa treatment. Widemouth Bay, Bude EX23 0DE. Open daily midday–2, 6–9 01288 361207. www.widemouthmanor.co.uk

THE EXTRA STEP

Robert Hawker and the Cornish anthem

Just up the coast from Poundstock, past the seaside resort of Bude and in an Area of Outstanding Natural Beauty, lies Morwenstow – the most northerly parish in the county and the birthplace of the Cornish anthem.

In the 19th century, this coastal hamlet was home to an Anglican priest and poet by the name of Robert Hawker, who wrote *The Song of the Western Men* (better known as *Trelawney*), the county's anthem. Hawker submitted the piece anonymously to a Plymouth newspaper, but was later recognised for his work by Charles Dickens in the serial magazine *Household Words*.

Hawker was something of an eccentric, who wore brightly coloured clothes and loved nothing more than to gaze for hours out to sea. In fact, the man spent so much of his time on the clifftops here that he built himself a little hut from driftwood into the face of the cliff. He spent many hours in contemplation in this hideaway, writing hymns and poems, smoking opium and entertaining guests, one of whom was Alfred Lord Tennyson. Today, Hawker's Hut is the smallest property owned by the National Trust.

Another facet of the priest's curious character was his obsession with shipwrecks and their victims. Parson Hawker, as his parishioners knew him, was usually the first person to rush to the shore when a boat ran aground. He also fought a popular superstition that bodies of dead sailors washed up on the beaches should be returned to the sea, arguing their right to a Christian burial.

During Hawker's time in the parish, he buried 40 or so corpses of seamen in the churchyard, five of which had been on board the cargo ship the *Caledonia*, which sank in 1842. The priest nursed the ship's sole survivor back to health, and the two became lifelong friends as a result of the experience. A model of the ship's white figurehead stands in the graveyard as a memorial to its unfortunate crew; the original is now kept in the church, in an effort to preserve it. Jeremy Seal's informative investigation into the event, *The Wreck at Sharpnose Point: A Victorian Mystery*, explores alternative perspectives on this fascinating story.

Before you leave the parish, the mismatching vicarage chimneys deserve your attention. Yet more evidence of Hawker's quirkiness, these were built to match the towers of various churches associated with the priest, as well as, in the case of the one above the kitchen, his mother's tomb.

…ST WALKS FOR...

...SUNSETS

C.01 West Penwith
C.06 Newquay & West Pentire
C.12 Fox Tor & East Moor
C.13 Trebarwith & Tregardock

...LONG HIKES

C.01 West Penwith
C.03 Black Head
C.05 Godrevy
C.13 Trebarwith & Tregardock

...NATURE

C.02 Loe Valley
C.09 St Winnow & Lerryn
C.11 Blisland
C.14 Boscastle

...SWIMMING & SUNBATHING

C.02 Loe Valley
C.06 Newquay & West Pentire
C.08 Lansallos & Lantivet Bay
C.13 Trebarwith & Tregardock

...BREATHTAKING VIEWS

C.01 West Penwith
C.05 Godrevy
C.07 Dodman Point & Gorran Haven
C.11 Blisland

...FAMILIES

C.07 Dodman Point (shortcut route)
C.09 St Winnow & Lerryn (shortcut route)
C.10 Cadson Bury Hill
C.11 Blisland (shortcut route)

...PITSTOPS

C.01 West Penwith
C.06 Newquay & West Pentire
C.09 St Winnow & Lerryn
C.11 Blisland

...CHALLENGING HILLS

C.01 West Penwith
C.11 Blisland
C.13 Trebarwith & Tregardock
C.14 Boscastle

Please

Shut The Gate

ABOUT THE AUTHOR

Rob Smith, founder of the *Secret Seeker* guidebook series, has always had a love of walking which stems from long summer holidays spent in southwest England as a child. In his late teens, he moved to France to follow his passion for cooking, working his way up from *plongeur* to chef at a variety of restaurants. He travelled leisurely from Provence to Paris before returning to the UK in 1996 to establish *The Shoreditch Map.* This monthly listings magazine, for which he wrote about venues and events across the stylish London neighbourhood, ran for over 80 issues before he passed it on as a successful enterprise.

These days Rob divides his time between London and Ibiza, where he works on book production and design, delegating the field work to researchers, editors, photographers and writers. Travelling to research locations to check the work of researchers and writers is a welcome break from the office-based work on production.

Rob hopes that his fledgling publishing company will grow and the books he publishes will gain a keen following of users who appreciate handpicked and carefully researched content, as well as good design and evocative writing. Keep your eye on secretseeker.com for more books in the series.

ACKNOWLEDGEMENTS

As well as the kind help and hospitality of the people of Cornwall, Rob would like to pass on his profound gratitude to the following people.

Alex Whittleton and Katie Halpin, faultless editors who worked tirelessly on the words and content. Steve Marvell and John Payne for their excellent contributions to the research and the Extra Step articles, respectively. Ben Hoo and Nicola Erdpresser – Ben for the overall design and Nicola for the solid desktop publishing. Brendan Barry for the outstanding and inspiring photography. And, finally, Jo Kirby and Becky Fountain for guidance, advice, proofing and much-needed support.